FIELD GUIDE TO

MICROSOFT
EXCEL
FOR WINDOWS 95

PUBLISHED BY

Microsoft Press
A Division of Microsoft Corporation
One Microsoft Way
Redmond, Washington 98052-6399

Library of Congress Cataloging-in-Publication Data
Nelson, Stephen L., 1959-
   Field guide to Microsoft Excel for Windows 95 / Stephen L. Nelson.
      p.   cm.
   Includes index.
   ISBN 1-55615-839-4
   1. Microsoft Excel for Windows. 2. Business -- Computer Programs.
3. Electronic spreadsheets. I. Title.
HF5548.4 .M523N4524 1995
650'.0285'5369--dc20   95-24059
                                             CIP

Printed and bound in the United States of America

1 2 3 4 5 6 7 8 9 BPress 9 8 7 6 5

Distributed to the book trade in Canada by Macmillan of Canada, a
division of Canada Publishing Corporation.

A CIP catalogue record for this book is available from the British Library.

Microsoft Press books are available through booksellers and distributors
worldwide. For further information about international editions, contact
your local Microsoft Corporation office. Or contact Microsoft Press
International directly at fax (206) 936-7329.

Macintosh is a registered trademark of Apple Computer, Inc. Quattro Pro
is a trademark of Borland International, Inc. 1-2-3 and Lotus are
registered trademarks of Lotus Development Corporation. WordPerfect is
a registered trademark of Novell, Inc.

Acquisitions Editor: Lucinda Rowley
Project Editor: John Pierce
Technical Contact: Mary DeJong

FIELD GUIDE TO

MICROSOFT
EXCEL
FOR WINDOWS 95

Stephen L. Nelson

The Field Guide to Microsoft Excel version 7 is divided into four sections. These sections are designed to help you find the information you need quickly.

ENVIRONMENT

Terms and ideas you'll want to know to get the most out of Excel. All the basic parts of Excel 7 are shown and explained. The emphasis here is on quick answers, but most topics are cross-referenced so you can find out more if you want to.

Diagrams of key windows components, with quick definitions, cross-referenced to more complete information

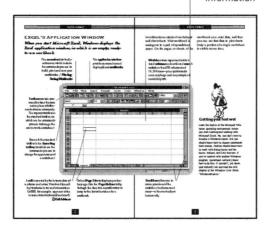

Tipmeister

Watch for me as you use this Field Guide. I'll point out helpful hints and let you know what to watch for.

Step-by-step guides to performing most Excel tasks

Quick identification of icons and groups

Definitions of key concepts and terms, and examples of why you should know them

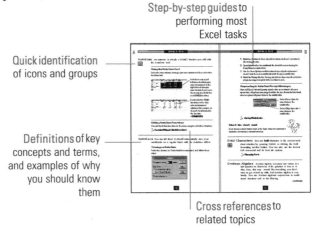

Cross references to related topics

INTRODUCTION

●●●

In the field and on expedition, you need practical solutions. Fast. This Field Guide provides just these sorts of lightning-quick answers. But take two minutes and read the Introduction. It explains how this unusual little book works.

WHAT IS A
FIELD GUIDE ?

Sometime during grade school, my parents gave
me a field guide to North American birds. With its
visual approach, its maps, and its numerous
illustrations, that guide delivered hours of
enjoyment. The book also helped me better
understand and more fully appreciate
the birds in my neighborhood. And the small
book fit neatly in a child's rucksack.

But I'm getting off the track.

This book works in the same way as that field guide. It organizes information visually with numerous illustrations. And it does this in a
way that helps you more easily understand and enjoy working with
Microsoft Excel.

For new users, the field guide provides a visual path to the information necessary to start using Excel. But the field guide isn't only for
beginners. For experienced users, the field guide provides concise,
easy-to-find descriptions of Excel tasks, terms, and techniques.

HOW TO USE
THIS BOOK

Let me explain how to find the information you need. You'll usually
want to flip to the first section, Environment, which is really a visual
index. You find the picture that shows what you want to do or the
task you have a question about. If you want to build a worksheet, for
example, you flip to pages 4 and 5, which show a worksheet.

Next, you read the captions that describe the parts of the picture—or
the key elements of Excel. Say, for example, that you want to build a
sales budget. The worksheet on pages 4 and 5 includes captions that
describe how to enter textual descriptions and budgeted values. These
key elements appear in **boldface** type to make them stand out.

You'll notice that some captions are followed by little paw
prints and **boldface** terms. These refer to entries in the second section, Excel A to Z, that provide more information related to the caption's contents. (The paw prints show you how
to track down the information you need. Get it?)

Excel A to Z is a dictionary of more than 200 entries that define terms and describe tasks. (After you've worked with Excel a bit or if you're already an experienced user, you'll often be able to turn directly to this section.) So, if you have just read the caption that says you can enter **formulas** into a worksheet, you can flip to the Formulas entry in Excel A to Z.

Any time an entry in Excel A to Z appears as a term in another entry, I'll **boldface** it the first time it appears in the entry. For example, as part of describing how formulas work, I might tell you that formulas can use a **cell address**. In this case, the words **cell address** will appear in bold letters—alerting you to the presence of a Cell Address entry in the second section. If you don't understand the term or want to do a bit of brushing up, you can flip to the entry for more information.

The third section, Troubleshooting, describes problems that new or casual users of Excel often encounter. Following each problem description, I list one or more solutions that you can employ to fix the problem.

The fourth section, Quick Reference, describes each of the menu commands and the tools (buttons) on the Standard, Formatting, and Chart **toolbars**. If you want to know what a specific command or command button does, turn to the Quick Reference. (And don't forget about the index. You can look there to find all references in this book to any single topic.)

CONVENTIONS USED HERE

One final thing I should tell you is this: Rather than use wordy phrases such as "Activate the File menu and then choose the Print command," I'm just going to say, "Choose the File Print command." Rather than say, "Choose the Format Painter toolbar button from the Standard toolbar," I'm going to say, "Click the Format Painter tool." (I'll show a picture of the toolbar button in the margin, too.) I also assume you know how to select menu commands, windows, and dialog box elements using either the mouse or the keyboard. No muss. No fuss.

ENVIRONMENT

Need to get the lay of the land quickly? Then the Environment is the place to start. It defines the key terms you'll need to know and the core ideas you should understand as you begin exploring Microsoft Excel.

EXCEL'S APPLICATION WINDOW

When you start Microsoft Excel, Windows displays the Excel application window, which contains an empty, ready-to-use workbook.

The menu bar lists the Excel menus, which include the commands you use to build, print, and save your workbooks.
❖ Printing; Saving Workbooks

The application window provides a menu bar and displays Excel **workbooks**.

Toolbars contain command buttons that you use in place of often-needed menu commands. The topmost toolbar is the Standard toolbar, on which are the commands you use to change the contents of a worksheet.

Beneath the Standard toolbar is the Formatting toolbar. It contains the commands you use to change the appearance of a worksheet.

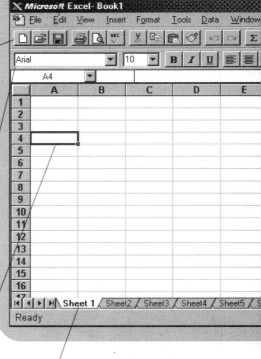

A cell is created by the intersection of a column and a row. You identify a cell by its column letter and row number. Cell B5, for example, appears at the intersection of column B and row 5.
❖ Cell Address

Select **Page Tabs** to display a particular page. Use the Page Buttons to flip through the sheets in a workbook or to jump to the first or last sheet in a workbook.
❖ Sheet Names

Workbooks are stacks of worksheets and chart sheets. A workbook is analogous to a pad of spreadsheet paper. On the pages, or sheets, of the workbook, you enter data, and then you can use that data to plot charts. Only a portion of a single worksheet is visible at one time.

Worksheets are organized into lettered **columns** and numbered **rows**. A worksheet has 256 columns and 16,384 rows—plenty of room for even very large and very complex financial reports.

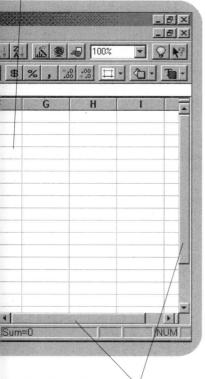

Getting your feet wet

Learn the basics of Microsoft Windows 95 before you start learning and working with Microsoft Excel. No, you don't need to become a Windows 95 expert. But you should know how to choose commands from menus. And you should know how to work with dialog boxes and the boxes, buttons, and lists they use. If you've worked with another Windows 95 program, you almost certainly know how to do this. If you don't, put down your butterfly net and read the first few chapters of your Windows 95 documentation.

Scroll bars allow you to move your view of the worksheet's columns and rows—either vertically or horizontally.

MICROSOFT EXCEL WORKSHEETS

Worksheets are the basic building blocks of workbooks. By entering information for labels, values, and formulas into worksheet cells, you create tables, or spreadsheets, useful for summarizing, tabulating, and analyzing.

Formulas can add, subtract, multiply, and divide values. Usually, these values are stored in another cell. To get a value stored in a cell, the formula uses the cell's address. This formula adds the values in cells B9, B10, B11, B13, B14, and B15.

Labels are pieces of text. Often, you use labels to describe values stored in other cells.

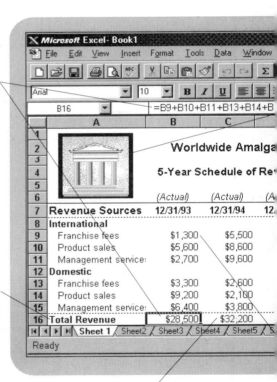

Numeric punctuation— dollar signs, commas, and decimal places—makes worksheet values easier to read.

❖ Formatting

To build a worksheet, you simply enter **labels, values,** and **formulas** into the cells. To do this, click on the cell, type what you want, and then press Enter. The unique feature of a spreadsheet program such as Microsoft Excel is its ability to calculate formulas.

When you enter a formula into a worksheet cell, Excel calculates the formula's result. If the formula uses values from other cells—the usual case—Excel recalculates the formula's result any time one of these values changes.
❖ Calculating Formulas

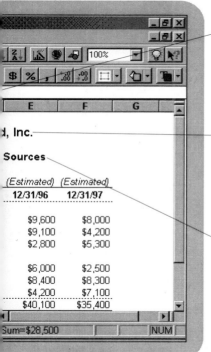

You can add pictures—such as a company logo—to worksheets if the picture is stored on disk as a graphic image. To do this, choose Insert Picture.
❖ Worksheet Pictures

Row heights and column widths can be adjusted to make space for long labels and large values.
❖ Columns; Rows

Type style and size can be used to make characters and numbers in labels and values easier to read. You can also add border lines.
❖ Borders; Fonts; Points

Values are numbers you want to use in formulas. You also use values to represent dates.
❖ Date Values

Quick and easy formatting

One easy way to add **formatting** is with the Format AutoFormat command. Simply select the worksheet area, or range, choose Format AutoFormat, and select a format.

5

MICROSOFT EXCEL CHARTS

Using Excel's ChartWizard, you can quickly create charts that visually depict worksheet data. Charts appear either as objects embedded in a worksheet or on their own workbook sheet.

A data category is the method you use to organize **data series** values. Usually, these are simply the time periods you use to plot the data series. Here, for example, the data category is years.

	A	B	C	D
		1991	1992	1993
2	15-year fixed-rate mortgages	7.3%	6.8%	6.3%
3	30-year fixed-rate mortgages	7.8%	7.3%	6.8%
4	30-year adjustable-rate mortgages	5.4%	5.1%	4.7%
5	15-year adjustable-rate mortgages	5.8%	5.4%	5.1%

The sets of related values you plot are called data series. This worksheet shows four "interest rate" data series: 15-year fixed-rate mortgages, 30-year fixed-rate mortgages, 15-year adjustable-rate mortgages, and 30-year adjustable-rate mortgages.

Different chart types use different data markers: bars, pie slices, lines, and so on. You can easily change the chart type by using the Chart toolbar or the Format Chart Type command. Excel differentiates the data markers for each data series. For example, on this chart, columns appear in different shades of gray.

The value axis helps someone looking at the chart calibrate the plotted values. You can add value axis **gridlines** too.

To create a chart, you first build a worksheet that holds the data to be plotted. Then you select the data range (by dragging the mouse from the upper left corner to the lower right corner) and start the ChartWizard. So what does the ChartWizard do? It steps you through five dialog boxes that ask how Excel should plot your data.

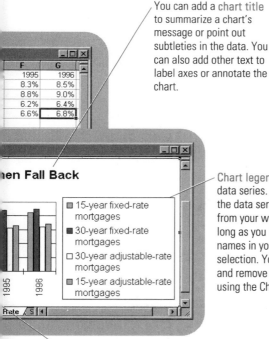

You can add a chart title to summarize a chart's message or point out subtleties in the data. You can also add other text to label axes or annotate the chart.

Chart legends name the data series. Excel will use the data series names from your worksheet as long as you include these names in your worksheet selection. You can add and remove chart legends using the Chart toolbar.

The category axis helps chart viewers keep the data organized. Excel will use category names from your worksheet as long as you include these names in your worksheet selection.

LIST MANAGEMENT

List Management is a simple yet handy database feature. A list is an organized set of similar chunks of information.

The first row names the fields of the list. Each column stores the same information: last names in column A, first names in column B, and so on.

To create a list, you use the rows and columns of a worksheet. In this example, each employee goes into a separate row: Peter Abbot on the first row, Shalandra Borchert on the second row, and so on.

🔅 Creating Lists

This list shows only 15 entries, or records, and uses only 5 columns, even though an Excel worksheet provides 16,384 rows and 256 columns. So you can store very large lists in a worksheet if your computer has enough memory and disk space.

Salaries

	A	B	C	D	E
1	**Last Name**	**First Name**	**MI**	**Department**	**Salary**
2	Abbot	Peter	W	Sales	$14
3	Borchert	Shalandra	P	Mfg	$18
4	Chang	Geng	Y	Mfg	$38
5	DeLaurenti	Anthony	L	Mfg	$34
6	Edwards	Jennifer	B	Sales	$3
7	Foles	Thomas	L	Sales	$8
8	Gonzalez	Rachel	MI	Sales	$40
9	Hapsburg	Jackson	A	Acctg	$8
10	Ito	Fumio	S	Acctg	$32
11	Johnson	Geoffrey	C	Acctg	$20
12	Kirkland	Ralph	E	Acctg	$47
13	Land	Walter	O	Admin	$22
14	Mercedes	Marie	C	Admin	$47
15	Nagai	Patrick	T	Mfg	$18

Sheet1 / Sheet2 / Sheet3 / Sheet4 / Sheet5 / Sheet6

You can arrange, or sort, list entries. For example, you can alphabetize a list by employee last names (as shown here). You can also organize a list in order of ascending or descending value fields (such as by salary).

🔅 Sorting Lists

To build a list, you use a worksheet. Typically, you use a row for each list entry. Information stored in a list can be textual (for example, employee names) or numeric (for example, salary amounts). You can also include formulas.

You can enter data directly into the worksheet by clicking a cell, typing, and pressing Enter, or you can use the Data Form command.

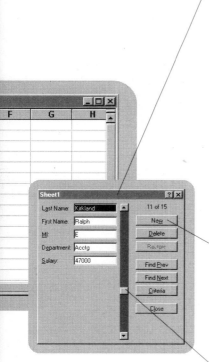

In the Data Form dialog box, you can enter and edit records in a list. To use it, select a list's headers and its entries and then choose the Data Form command. Excel uses the worksheet name to name the dialog box, and it uses the column headings to label the text boxes in the dialog box.

Click New to start a new entry with the Data Form dialog box, and then fill in the blank text boxes and move to the next record.

To edit the list entry displayed, edit the text box contents and move to the next record. You can page through the list using the Up arrow and Down arrow keys, the Find Next or Find Prev buttons, and the scroll bar.

PRINTING WORKBOOKS

You can print the worksheets and chart sheets as they appear on the screen. The same font styles and point sizes, border lines, and graphic images that appear on your screen will appear on the printed page.

You choose a page orientation that fits your worksheet or chart using the File Page Setup command's Page tab. Often, worksheets and charts fit better if the page orientation is "landscape," or horizontal, as shown here.

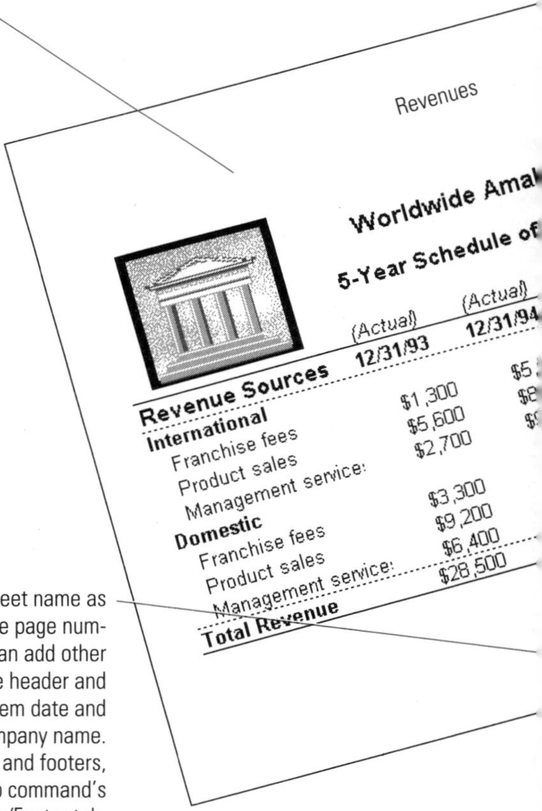

Revenues

Worldwide Ama▮

5-Year Schedule of

	(Actual)	(Actual)
	12/31/93	12/31/94

Revenue Sources		
International		$5,▮
Franchise fees	$1,300	$8▮
Product sales	$5,600	$9▮
Management service:	$2,700	
Domestic		
Franchise fees	$3,300	
Product sales	$9,200	
Management service:	$6,400	
Total Revenue	$28,500	

By default, Excel uses the sheet name as a page header and uses the page number as a page footer. You can add other bits of information to the header and footer too, such as the system date and printing time and your company name. To change page headers and footers, use the File Page Setup command's Header/Footer tab.

⁂ **Headers and Footers**

To print a worksheet or a chart, simply display it and then choose the File Print command. Excel displays a dialog box that asks what and how you want to print, but you can accept the default, or suggested, print settings by pressing Enter.

❧ Printing

Previewing printed pages

You can see what your printed pages will look like without actually printing them. Just choose the File Print Preview command. Excel displays a window that shows a printed page and provides command buttons you can use to page through the document, adjust page settings (such as margins and footers), and initiate printing once things look right.

❧ Print Preview

Setting page margins controls where Excel prints on a page and how much room is available for printing. You can also tell Excel to print small worksheets and charts in the center of a page's print area. To control page margin settings, use the File Page Setup command's Margin tab.

❧ Page Setup

EXCEL
A TO Z

Maybe it's not a jungle out there. But you'll still want to keep a survival kit close at hand. Excel A to Z, which starts on the next page, is just such a survival kit. It lists in alphabetic order the tools, terms, and techniques you'll need to know.

Absolute Cell Address

An absolute cell address is simply a **cell address** you use in a formula but don't want adjusted when the formula is copied.

Creating Absolute Cell Addresses

Make the column and row components of a cell address absolute by preceding them with a dollar sign. For example, to make the cell address A1 absolute, insert dollar signs—A1.

Creating Mixed Cell Addresses

In a mixed cell address, only some components are absolute. To create a mixed cell address, simply precede those address components you want absolute with a dollar sign. For example, the cell address $A1 has only its column fixed, and the cell address A$1 has only its row fixed.

The absolute key

When editing or entering a cell address, you can press F4 to change a cell address from relative to absolute, from absolute to mixed, and from mixed back to relative.

Copying Formulas; Relative Cell Address

Active Cell

The active cell is the cell with the **cell selector,** or pointer (that dark bordered thingamajig that jumps from cell to cell as you press direction keys). If you type something and press Enter, Excel puts what you type into the active cell. And the address of the active cell—the **cell reference**— shows in the Name box.

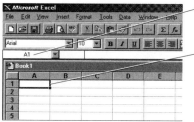

You can always tell which cell is active by looking at the Name box.

Excel also identifies the active cell with the cell selector.

Active Sheet   The active sheet is the one you can see in the workbook window. It's the sheet that selected commands act on. Note too, my friend, that the active sheet determines which menu bar Excel provides. For example, if a worksheet is active, Excel displays the worksheet menu bar; if a chart sheet is active, Excel displays the chart menu bar.

Active Windows   The active **application window**—such as the Excel application window—is the one that appears in front of all other open windows. (Cleverly, this is called the "foreground." The inactive application windows, if there are inactive applications, appear in the "background.")

The active workbook window is the one that any Excel commands you choose will affect. You can tell which workbook window is active because its title bar will show in a different color (usually blue).

Activating Document Windows

To activate a different workbook window, click the window or choose the Window menu command that names the window.

Activating Application Windows

To activate a different application window, click the window or use Alt+Tab to cycle through the open applications.

Adding Styles A style is a combination of formatting choices. To add a style to an open workbook, format a cell so that it uses the style, and then choose the Format Style command.

1 In the Style Name box, name the style.

2 The Style Includes box shows the formatting choices that make up the style. To remove formatting choices, unmark check boxes.

3 Click Add when the Style dialog box shows the formatting choices you want to combine as a style.

4 If you want to change a style, select it from the Style Name box, click Modify, and use the Format Cells dialog box that Excel displays.

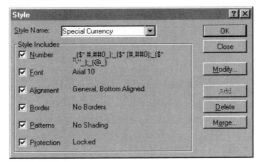

Deleting styles

If you inadvertently add a style you don't want or if you don't need a style anymore, select it from the Style Name box and then click Delete.

Formatting

Aligning Labels and Values
Alignment refers to how Excel positions **labels** and **values** in cells. Unless you tell it otherwise, Excel applies two simple alignment rules: left-align labels, and right-align values. You can override these rules with the Format Cells command. Follow these steps:

1 Select the cell or cells.

2 Choose the Format Cells command. Excel displays the Format Cells dialog box.

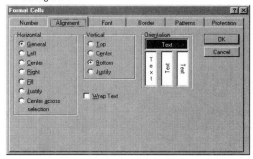

3 Select the Alignment tab. Excel displays the Format Cells Alignment tab options.

4 Use the Horizontal radio buttons to indicate how labels and values should align with the left and right edges of cells:

Choice	Result
General	The usual two rules are applied.
Left	Labels and values are left-aligned.
Center	Labels and values are centered between the left and right edges of cells.
Right	Labels and values are right-aligned.
Fill	Labels are repeated in a cell as many times as they will fit.
Justify	Row height is adjusted and labels are broken into multiple lines of text.
Center Across Selection	Labels and values are centered across the selected cells.

continues

Aligning Labels and Values *(continued)*

5 Turn on the Wrap Text check box if you want row heights adjusted and labels broken into lines of text. (This is sometimes called wordwrapping.)

6 Use the Vertical radio buttons to indicate how labels and values should be aligned with the top and bottom edges of cells:

Choice	Result
Top	Labels and values are aligned flush to top edge.
Center	Labels and values are centered between top and bottom edges.
Bottom	Labels and values are aligned flush to bottom edge.
Justify	Row height is adjusted so that labels can be broken into vertical lines of text.

7 Use the Orientation boxes to indicate how labels and values should appear in cells. (The boxes depict the alternatives.)

8 Click OK.

Answer Wizard Choose the Help Answer Wizard command to display the Answer Wizard tab in the Help dialog box. You can type natural-language questions here, such as "How do I find values in cells?" The wizard returns a short list of possible Help topics you can choose from. If **Help** isn't very helpful, just rephrase the question to get another list of topics.

Apple Macintosh This book isn't about Excel for the Macintosh. It's about Excel for Windows 95. But I want to tell you something you may not know: You can easily move spreadsheets from Excel for Windows 95 to Excel for the Macintosh. The reason for this is that an Apple Macintosh comes with a special application called Apple File Exchange. It converts IBM PC files, such as an Excel for Windows 95 workbook, to equivalent Mac files, such as an Excel for the Macintosh workbook.

I'm not going to describe how you do this. I just want you to know that this is possible and very easy. If you have questions, look up "Apple File Exchange" in the Apple Macintosh user documentation.

 Date Values

Application Window
The application window is the rectangle in which an application such as Excel displays its menu bar, **toolbars,** and any open workbook **document windows.**

Applying Styles
To apply, or use, a style, follow these steps:

1 Select the cells you want to format.

2 Choose the Format Style command. Excel displays the Style dialog box.

3 Select the style from the Style Name box.

4 If you don't want to use one of the formatting choices—Number, Font, Alignment, Border, Patterns, or Protection—unmark its check box.

5 Click OK.

Painting styles

You can copy a style from one cell to another by using the Format Painter tool. Select the cell with the style you want to copy. Click the Format Painter tool on the standard toolbar. Then select the cell or range to which you want to copy the style.

 Formatting

Argument
An argument is a unit of information, or an input, used in a function. Arguments can be **labels, values, cell addresses,** cell names, **formulas,** and even other **functions.** Arguments are enclosed in parentheses and separated by commas. For example, the function that calculates a monthly loan payment uses a minimum of three inputs— the interest rate, the number of monthly payments, and the loan amount. If the annual interest rate is 8 percent, the loan is $5000, and number of years of monthly payments is 3, you could enter the following function:

=PMT(.08/12,3*12,5000)   *continues*

Argument *(continued)*

The annual interest rate is 8 percent, or 0.08; so the monthly interest rate argument is 0.08/12—the annual interest rate divided by 12. The loan requires monthly payments over 3 years; so the payments argument is 3*12, which returns the number of monthly payments made over 3 years. The last argument, 5000, is the loan amount.

A handful of functions don't use arguments. For example, the function for calculating the mathematical constant pi. When a function doesn't use arguments, follow the function name with empty parentheses, as shown below with the pi function:

=PI()

Function Wizard

Array

An array is a set of numbers—such as those stored in a row or a column. You can use arrays in **array formulas** to return other arrays. For example, you can add the array 1, 2, 3 to the array 4, 5, 6, and you get a new array—5, 7, 9.

Array 1:	1	2	3
+ Array 2:	4	5	6
= Array 3:	5	7	9

This makes sense, right? The first number in Array 3, 5, is calculated by adding the first numbers in the two input arrays, 1 and 4. The second number, 7, is calculated by adding the second numbers in the two input arrays, 2 and 5.

Array Formulas

With handy and powerful array formulas you can write a single formula that makes several calculations. Sure, this sounds complicated, but a quick example will show you the basics of **arrays** and array formulas. Take a peek at the following chunk of worksheet. Suppose, for the sake of illustration, that you want to multiply the values in each row of column A by the values in each row of column B. Multiplying the account balance in column A by the interest rate in column B, for example, would calculate the interest.

Writing an Array Formula

To create an array formula that makes this calculation, take these steps:

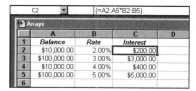

	A	B	C	D
	Balance	**Rate**	**Interest**	
1				
2	$10,000.00	2.00%	$200.00	
3	$100,000.00	3.00%	$3,000.00	
4	$10,000.00	4.00%	$400.00	
5	$100,000.00	5.00%	$5,000.00	
6				

C2   {=A2:A5*B2:B5}

1 Select C2:C5.

2 Type the equals sign, =.

3 Select A2:A5.

4 Type the multiplication sign, *.

5 Select B2:B5.

6 Press Shift+Ctrl+Enter.

Excel enters the formula {=A2:A5*B2:B5} into each of the cells in C2:C5. This array formula tells Excel, "Calculate C2 by multiplying A2 by B2, calculate C3 by multiplying A3 by B3, calculate C4 by multiplying A4 by C4, and calculate C5 by multiplying A5 by B5." By the way, the arrays in an array formula must have the same number of values.

Editing an Array Formula

You edit an array formula in the same way you edit other formulas. For example, double-click one of the cells with the array formula; then make your changes. If you edit an array formula, Excel removes the braces as you edit; so press Shift+Ctrl+Enter when you're done to tell Excel the formula is an array. By the way, when you edit one of the array formulas, Excel updates each of the formulas in the array.

About those braces

Note that you don't type the braces yourself to create an array formula; you press Shift+Ctrl+Enter, and Excel adds the braces for you.

 Array

ASCII Characters

The ASCII character set basically consists of the characters you see on your keyboard plus roughly a couple dozen other characters that you don't see, are unprintable, and you don't need to worry about anyway.

Excel provides text functions that manipulate ASCII characters, show which characters various ASCII codes represent, and show which ASCII codes return which characters.

As a general rule, you shouldn't have to worry all that much about ASCII characters if you're working with Excel. Why? You can type all the ASCII characters that you'll need with the keyboard.

ASCII Text Files

An ASCII text file is a text file that uses only **ASCII characters.** You can import one of these babies using the File Open command.

⁚⁚ Delimited Text Files; Importing Text Files

Auditing Worksheets

In a worksheet, which values get used where can be perplexing. To ease the burden, Excel provides a set of error-checking tools, which you make available by choosing one of the Tools Auditing commands: Trace Precedents, Trace Dependents, and Trace Error. These commands let you visually inspect relationships between **formulas** and the **values** used in formulas.

Tracing Precedents

The Auditing Trace Precedents command draws a blue arrow from the cells addressed by the active cell's formula to the active cell.

2	An input value	↑	1
3	Formula that uses input	↓	1

Tracing Dependents

You can see which cells depend on the active cell by using the Auditing Trace Dependents command. It draws a blue arrow from the active cell to cells addressing the active cell.

Tracing Errors

The Auditing Trace Error command draws arrows from cells addressed by an active cell's erroneous formula to the active cell. Excel draws red arrows from dependent cells holding error values; it draws blue arrows from all the other dependent cells.

| 6 | An erroneous input | #DIV/0! |
| 7 | Formula that uses input | #DIV/0! |

Two More Tools

Note that the Auditing submenu also provides two additional tools: Remove All Arrows, which erases the arrows you've added using the Trace commands, and Show Auditing Toolbar, which adds a toolbar for choosing auditing commands more quickly.

Dependents; Error Messages; Precedents

AutoCalculate AutoCalculate is pretty neat. You select a cell range, and AutoCalculate instantly calculates the values in the selected range. Six **functions** are available, AVERAGE, COUNT, COUNT NUMS, MAX, MIN, and SUM, with SUM as the default. Click the right mouse button on the AutoCalculate area to select the function you want to use.

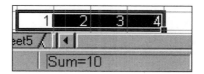

AutoCalculate shows the calculation result using the AutoCalculate area of the **formula bar**.

AutoCorrect AutoCorrect gets my vote for best new feature in Excel for Windows 95. AutoCorrect looks at the words you type and tries to fix all spelling and capitalization errors. For example, if you always misspell the word *the* as *teh*—perhaps your fingers fly just a bit too fast over the keys—AutoCorrect fixes your mistake. Automatically. Friends, I kid you not, it doesn't get much better than this.

AutoComplete When you type into a cell, AutoComplete scans all entries in the same column and determines if there is a possible match in the column. If so, AutoComplete fills in the rest of the entry for you. For example, if a cell contains the text entry "Nails," and you begin typing "N" in the cell below, AutoComplete fills in the rest of the entry, "ails." If there is more than one entry beginning with "N" in the column, AutoComplete fills in the entry as soon as the nearest match is found.

AutoComplete matches only complete cell entries, not individual words in a cell. As soon as a unique match is found, AutoComplete suggests an entry. AutoComplete does not work when editing formulas. AutoComplete only works in contiguous ranges of cells.

Getting picky about AutoComplete

If AutoComplete is enabled—and by default it is—you'll see a Pick From List command on the **shortcut menu.** (The shortcut menu appears when you right-click on a cell, as you might know.) Choosing the Pick From List command displays a list of all the unique entries in adjacent cells in the same column. Selecting one of the entries in the list inserts it in the selected cell. By the way, you can enable and disable AutoComplete by choosing the Options Tools command, selecting the Edit tab, and then marking and unmarking the Enable AutoComplete For Cell Values option.

Auto Fill ⁘ **Fill Series**

AutoFormatting Tables

You can format a worksheet selection, or range, to follow a conventional set of formatting rules. To do so, follow these steps:

1 Build the table and then select it.

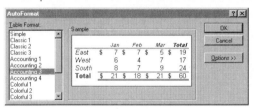

3 Year Plan	A	B	C	D	E
1		1994	1995	1996	
2	Revenue and Margins				
3	Revenues	100000	150000	225000	
4	Cost of Goods	35000	52500	78750	
5	Gross Margin	65000	97500	146250	
6	Expenses				
7	Administrative	10000	15000	22500	
8	Marketing	25000	37500	56250	
9	Research	50000	50000	50000	
10	Total Expenses	85000	102500	128750	
11	Profits	-20000	-5000	17500	
12					

2 Choose the Format AutoFormat command.

3 From the AutoFormat dialog box, select a format from the Table Format list box. Here I've selected the Accounting 3 format. The Sample box shows how the selected table format looks.

AutoFormat dialog box

	Jan	Feb	Mar	Total
East	$ 7	$ 7	$ 5	$ 19
West	6	4	7	17
South	8	7	9	24
Total	$ 21	$ 18	$ 21	$ 60

4 Click OK. The figure below shows an example worksheet range after using the Format AutoFormat command. Nice, huh? (This is the same worksheet range shown below step 1—only autoformatted using the Accounting 3 format.)

3 Year Plan	A	B	C	D	E
1		1994	1995	1996	
2	Revenue and Margins				
3	Revenues	$100,000.00	$150,000.00	$225,000.00	
4	Cost of Goods	$ 35,000.00	$ 52,500.00	$ 78,750.00	
5	Gross Margin	$ 65,000.00	$ 97,500.00	$146,250.00	
6	Expenses				
7	Administrative	$ 10,000.00	$ 15,000.00	$ 22,500.00	
8	Marketing	25,000.00	37,500.00	56,250.00	
9	Research	50,000.00	50,000.00	50,000.00	
10	Total Expenses	$ 85,000.00	$102,500.00	$128,750.00	
11	Profits	$ (20,000.00)	$ (5,000.00)	$ 17,500.00	
12					

AutoSum

An autosum is simply a SUM() function you insert with the AutoSum tool.

Using the AutoSum Tool

Select the row, column, or range you want to sum and then click the AutoSum tool.

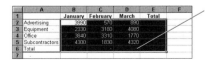

	A	B	C	D	E	F
1		January	February	March	Total	
2	Advertising	3990	570	890		
3	Equipment	2330	3180	4080		
4	Office	3640	3310	1770		
5	Subcontractors	4300	1830	4320		
6	Total					
7						

Include an empty cell below each column you want to sum and to the right of each row you want to sum. Excel uses these empty cells for the new SUM() functions.

	A	B	C	D	E	F
1		January	February	March	Total	
2	Advertising	3990	570	890	5450	
3	Equipment	2330	3180	4080	9590	
4	Office	3640	3310	1770	8920	
5	Subcontractors	4300	1830	4320	10450	
6	Total	14460	8890	11060	34410	
7						

Excel adds the SUM() functions to tally selected rows and columns. For example, in this cell, AutoSum adds the function, **=SUM(B2:D2)**

Editing AutoSum Functions

You edit AutoSum functions in the same way you edit other formulas.

🐾 **Function Wizard; Math Functions**

Bold Characters

B

You can **bold** characters in the current worksheet selection by selecting characters, then pressing Ctrl+B or by clicking the Bold tool. You can also use the Format Cells command and its Font tab options.

🐾 **Changing Fonts**

B

Boolean Algebra Boolean algebra, which you use in **conditional functions** and **filtering lists,** compares two values in a test question. If the test question answer is yes, the Boolean expression returns a 1. If the test question answer is no, the expression returns a 0. The following table shows and describes some typical Boolean expressions.

Test	Question it asks
A1=B1	Is value in A1 equal to value in B1?
A1>B1	Is value in A1 greater than value in B1?
A1>=B1	Is value in A1 greater than or equal to value in B1?
A1<B1	Is value in A1 less than value in B1?
A1<=B1	Is value in A1 less than or equal to value in B1?
A1<>B1	Is value in A1 not equal to the value in B1?

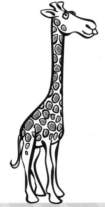

The problem of precedence

The comparison operators used in a Boolean expression have lower precedence than the other arithmetic operations—such as exponentiation, multiplication and division, and addition and subtraction. In other words, the comparison calculation is the last calculation made in a formula that uses a Boolean expression.

 Conditional Functions; Formulas

Borders

You can add border lines to cells. To do so, follow these steps:

1 Select the cell or cells.

2 Choose the Format Cells command. Excel displays the Format Cells dialog box.

3 Select the Border tab. Excel displays the Border options.

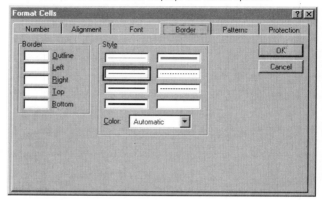

4 Use the Border options to choose on which cell edges the border should appear. Outline means around the outside edge of the cell selection, Left and Right mean along the left and right edges of every selected cell, Top and Bottom, well, you can guess this, right?

5 Use the Style options to choose border line thickness and make other line style decisions, for example, choosing dashes.

6 Use the Color drop-down list to select a border line color if you want something other than basic black.

AutoFormatting Tables

Calculating Formulas

Excel is very clever about the way it calculates **formulas.** Very clever indeed. It recognizes dependencies—so if one formula uses another formula's result, this other formula gets calculated first. Here's another clever twist. Unless you direct Excel to do otherwise, Excel recalculates your formulas whenever a formula or an input changes. (You won't always be able to tell when Excel recalculates formulas because it does so very quickly and in the background.)

If Excel is still recalculating a worksheet or if it needs to recalculate a worksheet, the word "Calculate" appears on the status bar. You can press F9 to manually tell Excel to recalculate.

Cell Address

A cell address identifies a specific cell by giving the cell's location using the column letter and row number. The cell address I81, for example, identifies the cell at the intersection of column I and row 81. U812 identifies the cell at the intersection of column U and row 812.

Cell addresses are mainly handy because you can use them in **formulas.** When you use a cell address in a formula, Excel retrieves the value stored in the cell and uses this value in the formula.

If you want to refer to a cell on another **worksheet** in the **workbook,** you need to precede the cell address with the sheet name and an exclamation point. Sheet2!B52, for example, identifies the cell at the intersection of column B and row 52 on Sheet2 of the workbook.

If you want to get really tricky and refer to a cell in another workbook, you need to precede the cell address with the workbook name in brackets, the sheet name, and an exclamation point. [BUDGET.XLS]Sheet2!B52, for example, identifies the cell at the intersection of column B and row 52 on Sheet2 of the workbook named BUDGET.XLS.

Cell Protection

Adding cell protection to a workbook hides cell contents and prevents changes to the cell contents. Adding cell protection requires two actions. First, you need to tell Excel which cells it should protect and how it should protect them. Second, you need to tell Excel to turn on this protection.

Identifying Protected Cells

To tell Excel which cells it should protect and how it should protect them, follow these steps:

1 Select the cells.

2 Choose the Format Cells command.

3 Select the Protection tab.

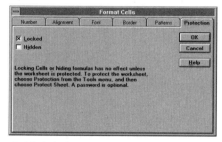

4 Mark the Locked check box to prevent changes to cell contents.

5 Mark the Hidden check box to prevent users from viewing cell contents on the formula bar. (The worksheet shows labels, values, and formula results; so do this to prevent users from viewing your formulas.)

6 Protect the worksheet as described in the next section, "Protecting a Worksheet."

C

Protecting a Worksheet

To turn on the protection in only the active worksheet, follow these steps:

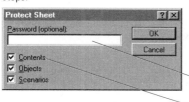

1 Choose the Tools Protection command.

2 Choose the Protect Sheet command.

3 If you want, add a protection password.

4 Use the Contents, Objects, and Scenarios check boxes to specify what you want to protect.

Unprotecting a Worksheet

To turn off worksheet protection, all someone needs to do is choose the Tools Protection Unprotect Sheet command. If you added a password, however, Excel will ask for the password before executing the command.

Protecting a Workbook

To turn on protection in all of a workbook's sheets, follow these steps:

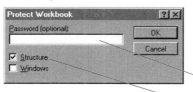

1 Choose the Tools Protection command.

2 Choose the Protect Workbook command.

3 If you want, add a protection password.

4 Use the Structure and Windows check boxes to specify what you want to protect.

Unprotecting a Workbook

To turn off workbook protection, choose the Tools Protection Unprotect Workbook command. If you added a password, however, Excel will ask for the protection password before executing the command.

 Passwords; Scenarios

Cell Reference   Cell reference is simply another name for **cell address.** I could, therefore, repeat the cell address definition given earlier, but let's save space instead. There are lots of cooler things to talk about.

Active Cell

Cell Selector   The cell selector is the square that Excel uses to mark the **active cell.** If you're confused by this, start Excel and look at your screen. Now fool around with the direction keys. See that thing that moves? That's the cell selector. Some people, by the way, call the cell selector a "cell pointer."

Changing Fonts   To change the **font** used for the selected cells' characters or the selected portion of text if you're editing a cell's contents, choose the Format Cells command. In the Format Cells dialog boxes, select the Font tab.

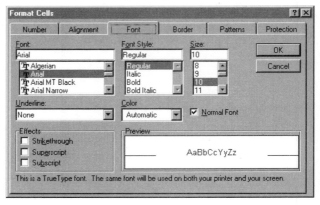

1 From the Font list box, select a font. Excel identifies printer fonts with the printer icon and identifies **TrueType** fonts with the ℡ logo.

2 In the Font Style list box, indicate whether you want regular characters, bold characters, or italic characters.

3 In the Size list box, select a point size. (One point equals 1/72 inch.)

4 Use the Underline drop-down list box to add underlining.

5 Use the Effects check boxes to specify other character effects, such as subscript.

6 Add color by using the Color drop-down list box. (Automatic means the Windows Control Panel controls color.)

7 Experiment with your font changes and then see their effect in the Preview box.

8 To return to the default, or suggested, font settings, mark the Normal Font check box. When you do, Excel sets the Font to Arial, the Font Style to Regular, the Size to 10, and the Color to Automatic. Excel also removes any underlining as well as any other special effects.

Making room for big characters

If you choose a larger point size, you may need to increase the row height to see the characters clearly.

Chart A chart is a picture that depicts worksheet data. In Excel you create these pictures-worth-a-thousand-words with the **ChartWizard.**

Adding gridlines to a chart ⁂ **Chart Gridlines**
Adding legends to a chart ⁂ **Chart Legends**
Adding titles to a chart ⁂ **Chart Titles**
Annotating charts with text ⁂ **Chart Text**
Changing chart colors ⁂ **Chart Colors**
Choosing a chart type ⁂ **Chart Types**
Creating a chart ⁂ **Chart Wizard**
Specifying how charts print ⁂ **Chart Page Setup**

Chart Colors
You can change the color of most parts of a chart, if the chart is displayed on a separate sheet. (If the chart isn't displayed on a separate sheet because it's an embedded chart, first select it by double-clicking.)

Changing Chart Part Colors

1 Double-click the part you want to change.

2 Select the Patterns tab. The Patterns tab options provide settings you can use to change the selected chart part's colors.

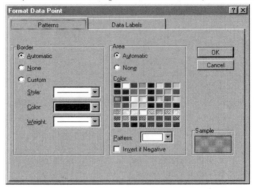

3 In the Border Color drop-down list box, select a color for the line drawn around the edge of the chart part—if the chart part has a border line.

4 In the Area Color option box, select the background color for the chart part.

I just want that one

To select a single **data marker** rather than all the data markers in the series, click the data marker twice.

Editing Embedded Charts

Chart Gridlines

You can use chart gridlines to make it easier to calibrate the values plotted in a chart and to differentiate the categories.

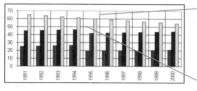

Category axis gridlines extend perpendicularly from the category axis—and help you keep the data categories straight.

Value axis gridlines extend perpendicularly from the value axis—and help you more easily calibrate plotted values.

Adding Horizontal Gridlines

To add horizontal gridlines to a chart, click the Horizontal Gridlines tool on the Chart toolbar.

Adding Value and Category Axis Gridlines

To add both value axis and category axis gridlines, choose the Insert Gridlines command.

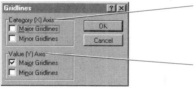

1 Use the Category (X) Axis check boxes to add or remove category axis gridlines.

2 Use the Value (Y) Axis check boxes to add or remove value axis gridlines.

Distinguishing between major and minor gridlines

Major gridlines extend from all the major tickmarks. Minor gridlines extend from all the minor tickmarks. Tickmarks are those little lines, or dashes, that intersect the axis.

Chart Legends

You use chart legends to name the **data series** plotted in a chart. Assuming you were either lucky or astute enough to include the data series names in your chart data selection, you can add a chart legend by clicking the Chart toolbar's Legend tool.

continues

Chart Legends *(continued)*

Unfortunately, if you don't include the data series names in your chart data selection, Excel doesn't know what to name the series. So it simply uses names such as Series1, Series2, and so on. Pretty boring, right? For this reason, it's a good idea to include data series names in your chart data selection.

 **ChartWizard; Data Categories**

Chart Page Setup
Choose the File Page Setup command and choose the Chart tab to display the dialog box you use to specify how charts print. (For this tab to appear, the active sheet must display a chart. If a chart is embedded, first double-click the chart to select it.)

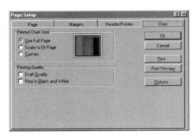

Changing the Chart Size

Use the Printed Chart Size radio buttons to control size. Mark Use Full Page if Excel should size the chart so that it uses the entire page. Mark Scale To Fit Page if Excel should print the chart so that it's as large as will fit on the page but still use the same ratio of height to width as the chart on your screen. Mark Custom if you want to print the chart using the on-screen dimensions.

Changing the Print Quality

Mark the Draft Quality check box to indicate that you want Excel to print faster at a lower resolution. Mark the Print In Black And White check box if you want Excel to print in black even though your printer outputs color.

 Printing

Chart Sheets Excel charts appear either as objects embedded in a worksheet or as separate workbook sheets. When you use the **ChartWizard** tool or the Insert Chart On This Sheet command to create a new chart, Excel embeds a chart object in the active worksheet. But you can place the chart on its own sheet by using the Insert Chart As New Sheet command.

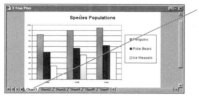

When you use the Insert Chart As New Sheet command, Excel starts the ChartWizard. The chart you create gets placed on a new sheet.

Chart Text You can annotate charts by adding text.

Adding Chart Text

To add text to a chart, display the chart's sheet or double-click the embedded chart, press Esc to be sure that nothing is selected, and then begin typing. To put the text onto separate lines, press Ctrl+Enter at the point where you want a line to end. Excel places your text in roughly the middle of the chart's plot area. You can move the text by selecting its box and dragging.

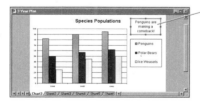

This is the chart text.

Formatting chart text

You can format chart text and **chart titles** in the same ways that you format cell contents. To format chart text, select the text and then choose the Format Selected Object command. To format chart titles, select the title and then choose the Format Selected Chart Title command.

Chart Titles You can add text to charts that names the chart and describes the axes. The easiest way to do this is to use the **ChartWizard** when you create the chart. To modify an existing chart, first display the chart's sheet if it has its own sheet or select the chart if it's embedded. Next choose the Insert Titles command, mark the Chart Title check box, press Enter, type the title text, and press Enter again.

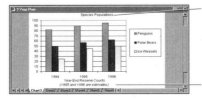

A chart title appears above the chart—and usually describes the chart's visual message or summarizes the data.

Axis titles appear next to the horizontal and vertical axes and describe what's being plotted.

Using different fonts in the same chart text

Look closely at the category title in the preceding chart and you'll see that the first line is in **bold** and that the second line is in *italic*. To format a chunk of title or text differently, select a portion of the text and use the Format Selected Object/Selected Title command. (The command name might be different, depending on what you select.)

Chart Types Excel supplies 14 chart types. You can choose a chart type when you create the chart, and you can change the selected chart's type by using the Format Chart Type command. Which method you use depends on the visual comparison you want.

Type	What chart shows
	Area charts plot data series as cumulative lines. The first data series values are plotted in a line. Then the second data series values are plotted in a line that gets stacked on top of the first line. Then the third data series values get stacked on top of the second line, and so on.

Type   **What chart shows**

A *Bar chart* plots each data series' values by using horizontal bars. Good for comparing individual values when the chart data category isn't time.

A *Column chart* is like a bar chart, but it plots each data series' values as vertical bars. Good for comparing individual values when the chart data category is time.

A *Line chart* plots each data series' values as points on a line. Emphasizes trends in the data series values.

A *Pie chart* plots a single data series with each value in the series represented as a pie slice. Probably the least effective chart type available because you're technically limited to a single data series and practically limited to a small number of values. (Otherwise you slice the pie into too many pieces.)

A *Doughnut chart* plots data series in rings, with each value in the series represented as a segment (bite) of the ring (doughnut).

Radar charts plot data series values using a separate value axis for each category. Value axes radiate from the center of the chart.

An *XY,* or *Scatter, chart* uses two value axes gridlines to plot pairs of data points in a line. Because it visually shows the correlation between two data series, this is the most powerful and useful chart type available.

continues

Chart Types *(continued)*

Type	What chart shows
3-D Area	Like its two-dimensional cousin, the *3-D Area chart* plots data series with lines and then colors the area between the lines. Note that some of the 3-D area chart autoformats use depth to organize the data series.
3-D Bar	A *3-D Bar chart* plots each data series' values using horizontal solid bars. Good for comparing individual values when the chart category isn't time—but a bit imprecise.
3-D Column	A *3-D Column chart* plots each data series' values as solid vertical bars. Note that some of the 3-D column chart autoformats use depth to organize the data series. Like the 3-D bar chart, a bit imprecise.
3-D Line	A *3-D Line chart* should probably be called a ribbon chart. It plots each data series' values as points on a ribbon. Emphasizes trends in the data series values, but tricky to use. (The ribbon's three-dimensionality makes it difficult to accurately gauge how fast the line rises or falls.)
3-D Pie	A *3-D Pie chart* plots a single data series with each value in the series represented as a pie wedge in a solid cylinder. Extremely difficult to use well. (Pie wedges in the chart background appear smaller than same-sized pie wedges in the foreground.)
3-D Surface	A *3-D Surface chart* plots data series as lines in a three-dimensional grid and then colors the surface between the data series. Often useful for creating rectangular data maps. (A data map plots values on a map using latitudinal and longitudinal coordinates.)

C

ChartWizard Excel's ChartWizard creates charts that visually depict workbook data. To use the ChartWizard, select the data you want to plot. (In your selection, include the data series names. Be sure to include the category names too if they appear in the worksheet.) Then follow these steps:

1 Click the ChartWizard tool. Excel changes the mouse pointer to a cross hair plus a small column chart.

2 Draw the box in which you want to place the chart. To do this, click on the upper left corner of the box, drag the mouse to the lower right corner, and then release the mouse button. Excel displays the first ChartWizard dialog box.

3 Confirm your chart data selection in the Range box and then click Next. Excel displays the second ChartWizard dialog box. (You can use the Back and Next buttons to move between ChartWizard dialog boxes.)

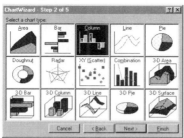

continues

ChartWizard *(continued)*

4 In the second ChartWizard dialog box, select a chart type by clicking its box. Click Next. Excel displays the third ChartWizard dialog
box.

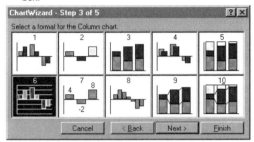

5 Select one of the chart styles, or autoformats, available for the
chart type. Click Next. Excel displays the fourth ChartWizard dialog
box.

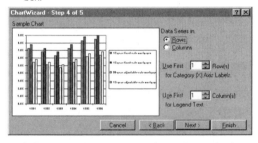

6 Indicate whether you arranged your data series by rows or by
columns.

7 Indicate which row holds the category names. (Excel knows
whether your category names are in a column or a row by looking
at the way you've arranged your data series. So this option's name
changes depending on the way you've arranged your data series.)

8 Indicate which column holds the data series names. (Excel knows
whether your data series names are in a row or a column by looking at the way you've arranged your data series too. So this
option's name changes depending on the way you've arranged your
data series.) Click Next. Excel displays the fifth (and final!)
ChartWizard dialog box.

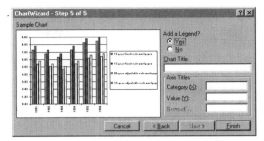

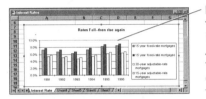

9 Indicate whether you want Excel to add a legend that names the data series and identifies their **data markers.** Excel places the legend to the right of the chart.

10 Type the text you want to appear above the chart. Type text you want to appear next to the categories axis or values axis. Then click Finish.

Excel embeds a chart like the one you've described in the active worksheet. An embedded chart floats on, or sits on top of, the worksheet holding the plotted data.

❖ Environment: Microsoft Excel Charts

Clip Art Clip art refers to the graphic images you can paste into documents. Although Excel doesn't come with any clip art, Microsoft Word for Windows does. (If you acquired Excel as part of Microsoft Office, you have Word for Windows and its clip art.) You can place clip art images into Excel workbooks as either pictures or objects.

❖ OLE; Worksheet Pictures

Clipboard Ever see the television show "Star Trek"? If you did, you may remember the transporter room. It let the Starship *Enterprise* move Captain Kirk, Mr. Spock, and just about anything else just about anywhere. The Clipboard is the Windows equivalent of the *Enterprise's* transporter room.

With the Clipboard, Windows easily moves just about anything anywhere. In Excel, you can use the Clipboard to move chunks of text, values, worksheet ranges, and even graphic images to and from different files. You can also use the Clipboard to move text, worksheet ranges, and even graphic images between Excel and other Windows applications such as Microsoft Word for Windows.

Using the Clipboard

To move information around via the Clipboard, you use the Edit menu's Cut, Copy, Paste, and Paste Special commands. So you don't have to know all that much about the Clipboard to make good use of it. One thing you should remember about the Clipboard, however, is that it stores what you've copied or cut temporarily. After you copy or cut, the next time you do so, the previous Clipboard contents are replaced. And when you exit Windows, the Clipboard contents are erased.

 **OLE; Sharing Microsoft Excel Data**

Closing Workbooks You close **workbooks** so that they don't consume memory, so that they don't clutter your screen, and so that they don't just plain annoy you.

Closing a Single Workbook

To close a workbook, click its Close button, or be sure the window is active and then choose the File Close command. The workbook's Close button appears at the right end of the menu bar for maximized workbook windows and in the upper right corner of unmaximized workbook windows.

C

Closing All Workbooks

To close all the open workbook windows at once, hold down Shift and then choose the File Close All command.

So you don't lose changes

If you've made changes to the workbook and haven't yet saved them, Excel asks if you first want to save.

Color

You can change the color of most parts of worksheets and charts.

Changing the color of border lines	**Borders**
Changing colors in a chart	**Chart Colors**
Changing the color of labels and values	**Fonts**
Changing cell background colors	**Patterns**

Coloring Worksheet Ranges

You can color a selected worksheet range by using the Color tool.

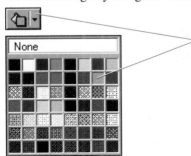

Click the down arrow next to the Color tool; then select one of the colors from the palette box that Excel provides.

Coloring Worksheet Text; Formatting

Coloring Worksheet Text
You can color the characters in a selected worksheet range by using the Font Color tool.

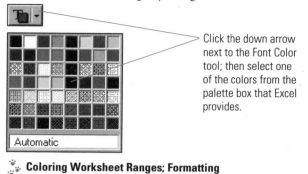

Click the down arrow next to the Font Color tool; then select one of the colors from the palette box that Excel provides.

Coloring Worksheet Ranges; Formatting

Columns
You can change the width of columns by using the mouse or with the Format Columns submenu commands. Using the mouse is easier. To change the width of a selected column or of several selected columns with the mouse, drag the edge of the column letter label.

Drag the edge of the column letter label left or right to change a column's width. Excel changes the mouse pointer to a two-directional arrow when you position the mouse on the column edge.

Rows

Conditional Functions
Conditional functions perform a logical test (described using **Boolean algebra**) and return a value or text string based on the results of the test.

Suppose, for example, that you're a teacher and that you want a formula that compares a student's final test score, the value in the cell named TestScore, with 60. If the student's test score equals or exceeds this value, the student passes. Otherwise, well, you get the picture. Here is an example conditional IF function.

=IF(TestScore>=60,"P","F")

This IF function compares the value in the cell named TestScore with 60. If the value in TestScore equals or exceeds 60, the function returns the one-character string P. If the value in TestScore is less than 60, the function returns the one-character string F.

Argument; Function Wizard

Converting Formulas into Numbers If you want to convert the **formulas** in a worksheet range to **values,** simply select the range that contains the formulas, choose Edit Copy, choose Edit Paste Special, mark the Paste Values option button, and click OK.

Copying You can copy and paste **values, labels,** formats, worksheet selections, and even graphic objects. You can do so within Excel or between Excel and another Windows application.

Copying data between applications	**Sharing Microsoft Excel Data**
Copying numeric formats	**Copying Cell Formats**
Copying values and labels	**Copying Data**
Copying worksheet formulas	**Copying Formulas**
Copying worksheet objects	**Copying Objects and Pictures**
Copying worksheet ranges	**Copying Ranges**

Copying Cell Formats
You can reuse the format of one cell for other cells.

Using the Format Painter Tool

One way—and often the easiest way—to copy formats is with the Format Painter tool. To do this, follow these steps:

1 Select a cell with the formatting that you want to reuse.

2 Click the Format Painter tool.

3 Select the cells you want to format.

You can also drag formatting

If you drag a cell or selection with the mouse's right button, Excel displays a shortcut menu of what I guess I'll call "dragging options." Choose the Copy Formats option to drag (copy) the formatting. If this sounds complicated, just try it.

Copying Formats with Commands

You can also copy cell formats by taking these steps:

1 Select the cell with the format you want to copy.

2 Choose Edit Copy.

3 Select the cell or cells in which you want to use the format.

4 Choose Edit Paste Special.

5 When Excel displays the Paste Special dialog box, click the Formats radio button in the Paste panel and click OK.

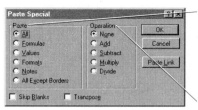

The Paste Special's Paste radio buttons let you control which features you've assigned to the cell get pasted into other cells and reused.

The Paste Special's Operation radio buttons let you specify whether pasted values should be combined in some way with the values already in the cells. Leave this set to None if you're pasting cell formats.

Copying Data
You can copy **values, labels,** and **formulas** between cells by using the mouse or commands.

Copying with the Mouse
To use the mouse, follow these steps:

1 Select the cell.

2 Hold down Ctrl and drag the selected cell's border to its new location.

Copying with Commands
To use the Edit Copy and Edit Paste commands, follow these steps:

1 Select the cell with the value or the label.

2 Choose Edit Copy.

3 Select the cell to which you want to copy the value or the label.

4 Choose Edit Paste.

⁘ **Clipboard; Copying Ranges; Drag-and-Drop; Fill Handle; Moving Data**

Copying Formulas
You can copy formulas between cells. The way you do this, however, depends on whether you want Excel to adjust any **relative cell addresses** used in the formula.

When Excel Should Adjust Formulas
If you want Excel to adjust the formula's relative cell addresses, you can copy a formula the same way you copy values and labels. For example, you can select the cell with the formula, hold down Ctrl, and drag it. Or you can select the cell with the formula, choose Edit Copy, select the cell to which you want to copy the formula, and choose Edit Paste. Either way, Excel adjusts the formula's relative cell addresses.

Deck Construction			
	A	B	C	D
1		Actual	Budget	
2	2 x 4s	35.67	40.00	
3	Plywood	76.42	80.00	
4	Nails	1.95	2.00	
5	Total	114.04		
6				

The formula =B2+B3+B4 adds the values in the cells above it.

Rather than reenter the same basic formula into cell C5, you can copy the formula in cell B5 to cell C5. Because the formula in B5 uses relative cell addresses, Excel pastes the formula =C2+C3+C4 into cell C5. *continues*

Copying Formulas *(continued)*

When Excel Shouldn't Adjust Formulas

If you don't want Excel to adjust the relative cell addresses used in the formula, you can make these relative cell addresses absolute (by editing the formula), or you can follow these steps:

1 Select the cell with the formula.

2 Click the **formula bar** and then select the formula (in the formula bar).

 3 Choose the Edit Copy command or the Copy tool.

4 Press Esc or click the formula bar's cancel button.

5 Select the cell to which you want to copy the formula.

 6 Choose the Edit Paste command or the Paste tool.

Absolute Cell Address; Copying Data; Moving Data

Copying Objects and Pictures To copy worksheet objects and pictures you've inserted, simply follow these steps:

1 Select the object or picture. Excel adds selection handles.

2 Hold down Ctrl.

3 Drag the picture to another location. (As you start to drag, Excel creates a new copy of the object or picture.)

Moving Objects and Pictures; Resizing Pictures; Worksheet Pictures

---

Copying Ranges You can use either the Edit Copy and Edit Paste commands or the mouse to copy a range.

Copying with the Mouse

To copy a worksheet range (and the **labels, values,** and **formulas** it holds) with the mouse, follow these steps:

1 Select the cells you want to copy.

2 Hold down Ctrl.

3 Click on the edge of the range.

4 Drag the selected range to the new location.

Copying with Commands

To copy a worksheet range with the Edit Copy and Edit Paste commands or the equivalent tools, follow these steps:

1 Select the cells you want to copy by dragging the mouse between the opposite corners of the worksheet range. Excel highlights the range to indicate it's been selected.

2 Choose the Edit Copy command or the Copy tool.

3 Select the upper left corner of the range into which the copied cells should be placed.

4 Choose the Edit Paste command or the Paste tool.

Automatic formula adjustments

When you copy a worksheet range, Excel adjusts the relative cell addresses used by any of the copied formulas.

⁙ **Copying Data; Copying Formulas;
Fill Handle; Moving Data**

Copying Sheets ⁙ Moving and Copying Sheets

Creating Lists To create a list on a worksheet, follow these steps:

1 Name the worksheet.

2 Enter the column headers, or field names, in the first worksheet row.

3 Select the header row and the next empty row.

4 Choose the Data Form command. Excel might display a dialog box that says it can't detect the headers. Click OK if you get this message.

5 Fill in the text boxes.

6 Click New to add an entry to the list.

7 Repeat steps 5 and 6 for every entry you want to add to the list.

⁙ **Environment: List Management**

Currency Symbols

Excel uses a currency symbol to punctuate monetary values that you format as currency. Which currency symbol Excel uses depends on the Control Panel's Regional Settings.

Changing Currency Symbols

To change the currency symbol Excel uses, click the Start button, then choose Settings Control Panel. Display the Regional Settings (by double-clicking the Regional Settings icon), select the Currency tab, and then enter a new currency symbol in the Currency symbol text box.

If you don't see the currency symbol you want to use on the keyboard, you'll need to enter the ANSI character code for the symbol. You do this by holding down the Alt key and using the numeric keypad to type the ANSI character code for the symbol. For example, hold down Alt and type 157 to enter the Japanese Yen symbol (¥). Hold down Alt and type 156 to enter the British Pounds Sterling symbol (£). (For other ANSI character codes, you need the Windows 95 *User Guide*.)

About Control Panel changes

Control Panel changes—for example, to the currency symbol—won't take effect until the next time you start Windows 95. To make your Control Panel changes take effect, close your applications and restart Windows 95.

 Formatting Numbers

Custom Filtering

The Data Filter command provides two methods for **filtering lists**. Often the quicker and easier method is to use the Data Filter AutoFilter command. You can also use the Data Filter Advanced command—if you're adventurous. (But you'll need to be clever enough to figure out how the command works without help from me.)

Databases ❖ List Management

Data Categories   Data categories organize the values in a chart's **data series.** This sounds confusing, but let me give you an easy rule of thumb. In any chart that shows how some value changes over time, data categories are time periods. So in a chart that plots sales over a 5-year period—say, 1992 to 1996—it's the years that are the data categories.

Data Markers   Data markers are the visual building blocks that Excel uses to draw a chart. Each Excel **chart type** uses a different data marker. A column chart, for example, has column data markers. A pie chart has pie-slice data markers. A line chart uses—no, wait a minute. You now know a line chart uses lines as data markers, right? One thing you may not know but may find interesting is that Excel also lets you use pictures as data markers.

❖ **Picture Charts**

Data Series   A data series is simply a set of related values plotted with the same **data marker** in an Excel chart. If you find the term *data series* confusing, you can use a sneaky trick to identify the data series that a chart plots. Ask yourself, "What am I plotting?" Every one-word answer will identify a data series. For example, if you ask the "What am I plotting?" question about a chart that plots sales revenue over 5 years, you can answer, "Sales." Sales, then, is a data series. By the way, the data markers that visually represent the set of sales values will all look similar. For example, the sales data series might be depicted with a set of red bars or as points along the same line.

❖ **Data Categories**

Date and Time Functions
Excel provides more than a dozen functions to make working with **date values** and **time values** easier. Using the DATE function, for example, you can easily determine the date value for a particular day. The function below returns the date value for December 31, 1996, which is 35430, by using as function arguments the year number (1996), the month number (12), and the day number (31):

=DATE(1996,12,31)

Argument; Function Wizard

Date Formats
Excel provides eleven date formats that you can use to make **date values** understandable.

Date Format Types
Here's a list of some of the ways Excel lets you format the date value 35366:

Type	Formatted date value
m/d/yy	10/28/96
d-mmm-yy	28-Oct-96
d-mmm	28-Oct
mmm-yy	Oct-96
m/d/y h:mm	10/28/96 12:00a

Formatting a Date
To format a date, select the cell or range with the date values. Then choose the Format Cells command and select the Date entry from the Category list. Finally, choose one of the date format entries from the Type list box.

Formatting Numbers; Time Values

Date Values

Excel lets you use values to represent dates: 1 to represent January 1, 1900, 2 to represent January 2, 1900, and so on, through 65380 to represent December 31, 2078. Of course, you don't want to have to remember which date the value 40000 represents; so Excel formats date values so that they look like dates.

This may all seem like much ado about nothing, but you can do some neat tricks with date values. Say you've got a workbook that keeps a record of invoices and estimates payment dates. If an invoice is due 30 days from the invoice date—for example, October 28, 1996—you can calculate the invoice due date by adding the value 30 to the date value for October 28, 1996 (35366). The formula result, 35396, gives the day you should expect payment. Of course, 35396 doesn't mean a whole heck of a lot to you or to me, but once you tell Excel to format this as November 27, 1996, things begin to look pretty clear.

Moving worksheets to the Apple Macintosh

If you move Excel workbooks between Windows and the **Apple Macintosh**, be forewarned: Excel for the Macintosh uses a different date value numbering scheme. On the Macintosh, the value 1 represents January 2, 1904. (If you want Excel for Windows to use the same date value numbering scheme as Excel for the Macintosh, choose the Tools Options command, select the Calculation tab, and mark the 1904 Date System check box.)

 Date Formats; Formulas; Time Values

Default File Location

If you want Excel to suggest a default location for the workbooks you save, follow these steps:

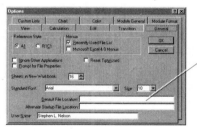

1 Choose the Tools Options command.

2 Select the General tab.

3 Enter the path name for the folder in the Default File Location text box.

4 Click OK.

Saving Workbooks

Default Fonts

Microsoft Excel, by default, uses 10-**point** Arial type for worksheets. To use another **font,** follow these steps:

1 Choose the Tools Options command.

2 Select the General tab.

3 Select the font from the Standard Font drop-down list box.

4 Select the point size from the Size drop-down list box.

5 Click OK. Restart Excel to have your new standard font style and size setting appear in workbooks.

Default Workbooks

Want a particular workbook to open every single time you start Excel? No problem. All you need to do is save the workbook in the XLStart folder of the Excel folder, which may be in the MSOffice folder.

Saving Workbooks

Deleting

You can remove—or delete—cells, charts, columns, rows, and worksheets.

Removing cells	**Deleting Cells**
Removing charts	**Deleting Sheets**
Removing columns	**Deleting Columns and Rows**
Removing rows	**Deleting Columns and Rows**
Removing worksheets	**Deleting Sheets**

Deleting vs. erasing

When you delete a cell, column, or row, it no longer exists in the worksheet. In other words, Excel physically removes the cell, column, or row, and then rearranges the worksheet so that there are no empty holes, or gaps. In comparison, when you clear, or erase, a cell, column, or row, Excel removes only the cell's contents and formatting.

Deleting Cells To delete, or remove, cells from a row or a column, select the cells and then choose the Edit Delete command.

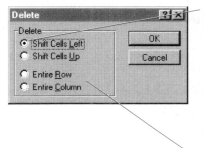

Use the Delete radio buttons to tell Excel how it should fill the "hole" left after the deletion: by moving up the cells in the selected column (indicated as Shift Cells Up) or by moving left the cells in the selected row (indicated as Shift Cells Left).

Don't use the Entire Row or Entire Column radio buttons unless you want to delete the selected cells' rows or columns.

Deleting Columns and Rows

Deleting Columns and Rows To delete columns or rows from a worksheet, select the columns or rows and then choose the Edit Delete command.

Deleting Cells; Editing Cell Contents; Error Messages

Deleting List Entries **Editing Lists**

Deleting Sheets To delete a **worksheet** or a **chart sheet,** display the sheet and then choose the Edit Delete Sheet command.

Delimited Text Files

A delimited text file is a file that uses a standard character—for example, the Tab character—to break apart the lines, or rows, of information. Excel's File Open command starts a wizard that helps you import text files, including delimited text files.

ASCII Text Files; Importing Text Files

Dependents

A dependent is a cell with a formula that references, or addresses, other cells. For example, if cell A1 uses the formula =B12+E6, it uses the values in cells B12 and E6. Cell A1, then, is a dependent cell, because it "depends on" cells B12 and E6.

Auditing Worksheets; Precedents

Dialog Box

A dialog box is simply an on-screen form you fill out to tell Excel how to complete a command. Any command name followed by an ellipsis (...) displays a dialog box.

Document Window

The document window is the rectangle that Excel uses to display your **workbooks.** If you have more than one workbook open, the **application window** will show more than one document window. I should probably tell you that some people call Excel's document windows "**workbook windows.**"

Counting the open document windows

The Window menu lists numbered commands for all of the open document windows. By activating the Window menu, you can learn how many and which document windows are open.

Drag-and-Drop
Drag-and-drop is a technique that lets you move and copy pieces of a **workbook** with the mouse.

Moving with Drag-and-Drop
To move some piece of a workbook—such as a cell, a range, or a picture—you select it and then drag it to its new location.

Copying with Drag-and-Drop
To copy some piece of a workbook—such as a cell, a range, or a picture—you select it, press Ctrl, and then drag it to its new location.

Drag-and-drop trick
If you drag a cell or range using the mouse's right button (instead of the left button), Excel displays a **shortcut menu** of commands you can use to copy or move the selection in a bunch of different ways.

Copying; Fill Handles; Moving Data

Drawing
Use the Drawing tool, which appears on the standard Excel toolbar, to draw objects such as arrows, circles, and rectangles by dragging the mouse. Click the Drawing tool to activate the Drawing toolbar shown below.

Click one of the Drawing tools on the first row of toolbar buttons, click where you want to start drawing, and then drag the mouse to draw whatever shows on the tool's face.

The second row of toolbar buttons provides command shortcuts for working with graphic objects.

Clip Art; Moving Objects and Pictures

Editing Cell Contents
To change the formula, value, or text stored in a cell, replace the cell's contents by entering some new formula, value, or piece of text into the cell. You can also double-click the cell so that Excel turns the cell into an editable text box. (That's "editable," not "edible.") Now make your changes.

You can also use the formula bar to edit the **active cell.** Simply click the formula bar, and Excel adds three buttons related to editing in the formula bar.

The formula bar shows the contents of the selected cell—in this case, a simple formula. It works like an editable text box.

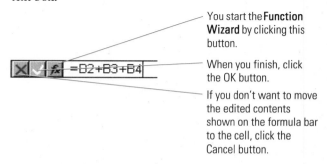

You start the **Function Wizard** by clicking this button.

When you finish, click the OK button.

If you don't want to move the edited contents shown on the formula bar to the cell, click the Cancel button.

Editing Embedded Charts
If you want to edit an embedded chart, double-click it. From the chart menu bar, use the Insert and Format menus to make additions, changes, and other what-have-yous. When you finish editing the chart, press Esc to redisplay the regular worksheet menu bar, or select a worksheet cell.

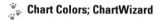 **Chart Colors; ChartWizard**

Editing Lists
To edit a list, select the list (including the column headings) and then choose the Data Form command. Make your changes in the Data Form dialog box.

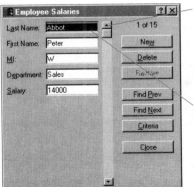

1 Use the scroll bar to display the list entry you want to change. (You can also use the Up arrow and Down arrow keys to move through the list.)

2 When the list entry is displayed, edit the text box contents.

3 Click Restore to undo your changes.

4 To delete the list entry shown in the dialog box, click Delete.

More about Restore

To reverse editing changes you've made to the list entry currently displayed, click Restore. Note, though, that you must click Restore before displaying another list entry. Also, Restore won't restore a list entry you've previously deleted.

Creating Lists; List Management; Searching Lists

Embedding and Linking Existing Objects
To create an object using an existing file, follow these steps:

1 Choose the Insert Object command.

2 Select the Create From File tab.

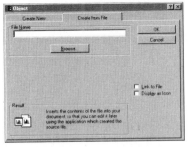

3 If necessary, click the Browse command button to open a dialog box that lets you root through your computer's disks and folders.

continues

Embedding and Linking Existing Objects *(continued)*

4 Use the File Name list box to identify the object file.

5 Mark the Link to File check box if you want Windows 95 to update the object for subsequent file changes.

6 Mark the Display as Icon check box if you want Excel to display an icon to represent the objects rather than a picture of the objects.

7 Click OK when you finish describing the embedded or linked object. Excel links or embeds the object into your Excel workbook.

⁘ **Copying Objects and Pictures; Moving Objects and Pictures; OLE; Resizing Pictures; Worksheet Pictures**

Embedding New Objects
To create an object from scratch using an application other than Excel, follow these steps:

1 Choose the Insert Object command.

2 Select the Create New tab.

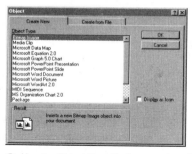

3 Use the Object Type list box to select the Windows-based application you'll use to create the object you are about to embed.

4 Mark the Display as Icon check box to see the embedded object as an icon rather than a picture of the embedded object.

5 When you click OK, Excel starts the selected application so that you can create the object. (To see the object in your Excel worksheet, use the selected application's File Update command.)

∵ **Embedding and Linking Existing Objects; OLE**

Entering Data   To enter a value or a piece of text in a cell, simply click the cell and then type whatever you want stored in the cell. You can enter **values, labels** (pieces of text), or **formulas** in this way. You can enter labels as long as 255 characters. You can enter values as long as 15 digits.

Predictable patterns

If you want to enter values that follow a predictable pattern, choose the Edit Fill Series command. What's a predictable pattern? Good question. Here are a couple of examples: a series of month-end date values, a set of numbers that increase by a set value (such as 1) or by a set percentage (such as 5 percent).

 ∵ **Fill Handle; Scientific Notation**

Erasing Cells   You can erase cell contents, formatting, and notes by using the Edit Clear submenu commands.

Erasing a Cell's Contents

To erase cell contents (meaning the stuff—values, labels, or formulas—stored in the cell), choose the Edit Clear Contents command or press Del.

Erasing Formatting

To erase cell formatting, choose the Edit Clear Formats command.

Erasing Cell Notes

To erase cell notes, choose the Edit Clear Notes command.

continues

Erasing Cells *(continued)*

Erasing Cell Contents, Formatting, and Notes

If you want to wipe out everything associated with the cell—its contents, it formats, and its **notes**—choose the Edit Clear All command.

The wrong way to erase

Don't remove a cell's contents with the spacebar. When you select a cell and then press the spacebar, you don't erase the cell's contents. Instead you replace the cell contents with a space character.

 Deleting; Deleting Cells; Formatting

Erasing Workbooks

Workbooks are files stored on disk. To erase them, therefore, you use either the Windows Explorer or My Computer's File Delete command. For information about how to use the Windows Explorer or My Computer to erase a workbook file, refer to the user documentation that came with your copy of Windows 95.

If you accidentally erase a workbook

You should know that it may be possible to recover, or unerase, a workbook file. If you've only recently deleted a file, you can retrieve it by opening the Recycle Bin and dragging the file to another folder. For more information on this, refer to Troubleshooting: You Accidentally Deleted a Workbook.

Error Messages

If a **formula** doesn't work right and Excel knows why, Excel will display one of the following error messages:

Message	The problem is that your formula
#DIV/0	Attempts the undefined operation of dividing by zero.
#NAME?	Uses a cell name you haven't defined or one you've misspelled.
#VALUE!	Tries to arithmetically manipulate some thing that's not a value—such as text.
#REF!	Addresses a cell or a range that doesn't exist—perhaps because you deleted it.
#NULL	Tries to return a value that doesn't exist.
#N/A	Addresses a cell that holds the "not available" code, #N/A.
#NUM!	Attempts some impossible mathematical operation such as calculating the root of a negative value.

 Auditing Worksheets

Exiting Excel

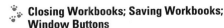 To exit from Excel—or just about any other Windows-based application—you can choose the File Exit command. Or you can close the Excel application window—for example, by clicking its Close button. Excel will ask if you want to save workbooks with unsaved changes.

Closing Workbooks; Saving Workbooks; Window Buttons

Exporting Exporting is copying a workbook so that you or a friend can use it with another spreadsheet or word-processor application. You can export an Excel workbook by saving a workbook in a file format that the other program can use.

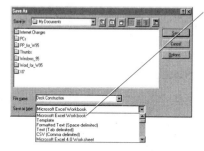

To export a workbook file, save the file in a format that the other program can open.

File Names You give a workbook its file name when you choose the File Save As command.

Choosing a File Name

Windows 95 file-naming rules apply to Excel workbook files. A file name can have as many as 256 characters. All numbers and letters that appear on your keyboard are OK. And so are many other characters. You can't, however, use characters that Windows 95 expects to be used in special ways, such as slashes, asterisks, and question marks. If you need more information than this, refer to the Windows 95 *User's Guide* that almost surely came with your computer or inside the Windows 95 packaging.

Choosing a File Extension

The Windows 95 file extension, by the way, isn't something you need to worry about. Windows 95 and Excel supply and use file extensions to identify file types. You can accept the default Microsoft Excel workbook file type, XLS, or you can use the File Save dialog box's File Type drop-down list box to select some other file type.

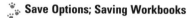 **Save Options; Saving Workbooks**

File Properties In addition to the worksheets and charts you store in a workbook, you can store additional information that describes the workbook itself and makes it easier to find. You collect and store this additional information by filling out the Summary tab of the workbook Properties dialog box, which Excel displays when you choose the File Properties command.

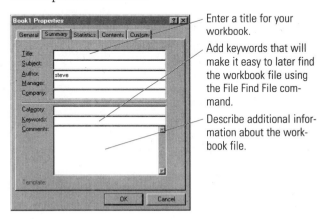

Enter a title for your workbook.

Add keywords that will make it easy to later find the workbook file using the File Find File command.

Describe additional information about the workbook file.

Fill Handle By dragging a fill handle with the mouse, you can fill a selected range with **formulas, values,** or **labels.** Or you can duplicate a pattern or a series (if Excel can figure out what the pattern or series is). I could spend pages describing how this works. But I think a better idea is for you to just noodle around with this a bit. Enter a value, label, or formula into a cell. Then drag the cell's fill handle up, down, left, right, and so on. You'll quickly see how the fill handle works.

This is the fill handle you drag. If you drag it right, Excel fills, or autofills, the cells with the names of the months.

continues

Fill Handle *(continued)*

A fill handle trick

If you drag a selection's fill handle using the right mouse button, Excel displays a **shortcut menu** of commands you can use to specify exactly what and how Excel should fill.

 Filling Cells

Filling Cells To fill a selected range with **formulas, values,** or **labels,** you can use the **fill handle,** as described above, or you can use one of the Edit Fill submenu commands, as described below.

Command	What it does
Edit Fill Down	Copies contents of the first, topmost row into the second and subsequent rows.
Edit Fill Right	Copies contents of the first, leftmost column into second and subsequent columns.
Edit Fill Up	Copies contents of the last, bottommost row into preceding rows.
Edit Fill Left	Copies contents of the last, rightmost column into preceding columns.
Edit Fill Across Worksheets	Copies contents of the first workbook sheet into second and subsequent worksheets.
Edit Fill Justify	Rearranges the active cell's label so that it evenly fills the selected cells.

 Fill Series

Fill Series Sometimes you'll want to fill cells with a series of **values** that fit a predictable pattern: only even numbers, for example, or month-end dates. Excel provides a special command, Edit Fill Series, which lets you do just this. To use the Edit Fill Series command, follow these steps:

1 Enter enough of the series' values to establish the pattern.

2 Select the cells with the values and those you want to fill.

3 Choose the Edit Fill Series command. Excel displays the Series dialog box.

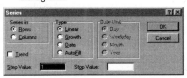

4 Indicate whether the series should be filled a row at a time or a column at a time.

5 Describe the pattern type:

Pattern	Description
Linear	Create the pattern by adding the step value to the preceding cell's value.
Growth	Create the pattern by multiplying the step value by the preceding cell's value.
Date	Create a date-based pattern as described by the Step Value and Date Unit option.
AutoFill	Create a pattern based on the first cell's value. (AutoFill copies formulas, and it linearly adjusts values by the step value.)

6 Enter the step value used to create the pattern.

7 Optionally, enter the stop value that terminates the pattern.

A fill series trick

You can drag a **fill handle** to fill cells with a series of values or labels, too. For example, if you drag the fill handle of a cell containing the label January, Excel fills the next cells with the labels February, March, April, and so on. For Excel to guess the series pattern, however, you may need to select a range of cells (so Excel knows the step value). This process is called "autofilling."

 Filling Cells

Filtering Lists
When you filter a list, you actually create a new list of entries that match a specified description.

Filtering an Existing List
1 Select the list.

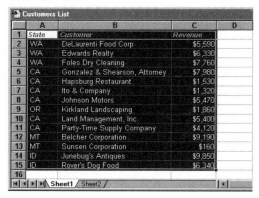

2 Choose the Data Filter AutoFilter command. Excel turns the header, or column heading, cells into drop-down list boxes.

3 Describe the list entries you want on your new list by activating the header, or column heading, drop-down list boxes and selecting a value. Or select one of the other entries, such as All, Blanks, NonBlanks, or Custom.

4 If you select Custom, Excel displays the Custom AutoFilter dialog box.

5 Use the operator and value drop-down list boxes to create a **Boolean algebra** expression that describes the filter; for example, =CA tells Excel you want list entries that show the state as CA.

F

Filtering with wildcards

When you enter **values,** you can use the ? character to represent any single character. And you can use the * character to represent any group of characters. The filter State=C? would return any 2-character state code starting with the letter C. The filter Customer=B* would return any customer name starting with the letter B.

6 Create compound AND/OR filters by marking the AND/OR radio buttons and using the second set of operator and value drop-down list boxes.

7 After you specify the filter, click OK. Excel creates a new list of only those entries that match the filter.

	A	B	C	D
1	State	Customer	Revenue	
5	CA	Gonzalez & Shearson, Attorney	$7,980	
6	CA	Hapsburg Restaurant	$1,530	
7	CA	Ito & Company	$1,320	
8	CA	Johnson Motors	$5,470	
10	CA	Land Management, Inc	$5,400	
11	CA	Party-Time Supply Company	$4,120	
16				

Creating a New List from a Filtered List

To create a new list using the filtered list, copy the filtered list to a new worksheet location.

Displaying an Entire List Again

Choose the Data Filter Show All command to, in effect, unfilter a previously filtered list.

Removing the AutoFilter Drop-Down List Boxes

Choose the Data Filter AutoFilter command. (Yes, again.)

Using Advanced Filters

The Data Filter menu's Advanced Filter displays a dialog box you use to identify the worksheet ranges holding the list and the filter descriptions (which need to be in the form of **Boolean algebra** expressions). I'm not going to describe this command here. Most people shouldn't ever need to use the Advanced Filter command.

Creating Lists; Sorting Lists

Financial Functions
Excel provides 15 financial functions for making depreciation expense calculations, for performing standard investment calculations such as the internal rate of return, and for calculating loan variables such as the periodic payment. For example, to calculate the monthly payment on a $10,000 loan with 60 months, or periods, of payments and a 1 percent per month interest rate, you can use the loan payment function shown below:

=PMT(.01,60,1000)

⁘ **Arguments; Function Wizard; Troubleshooting: A Financial Function Doesn't Work Correctly**

Finding Cells
Choose the Edit Find command to locate cells with specified contents: a fragment of text, part of a formula, a cell name or address, or a value.

Using the Edit Find Command
To use the Edit Find command, select the worksheet range Excel should search and then choose the command. If Excel finds a cell, it makes that cell active.

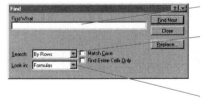

1 Specify what you're looking for.

2 Indicate whether Excel should search column by column or row by row.

3 Indicate where Excel should look: in formulas, at values, or in cell notes.

4 Click Find Next to start and restart the search.

Considering Case in a Search
Use the Match Case and Find Entire Cells Only check boxes to indicate whether Excel should consider case (lower vs. upper) in its search and look for entire cells rather than a portion of a cell.

⁘ **Replacing Cell Contents; Searching Lists**

Finding Files

You can use the File Find File command to locate workbooks based on characteristics of the file and summary information collected about the file. For step-by-step information on how to use this command to find a lost workbook, refer to **Troubleshooting: You Can't Find a Workbook.**

Fonts

You can use a wide variety of fonts in your worksheets. With fonts, you can even include Greek symbols and other special characters. Here are a few examples:

Clean and attractive, **Arial** resembles Helvetica.

Courier New looks like typewriter output.

Times New Roman uses serifs—little cross-strokes—to make characters easier to read.

 These are **TrueType** Wingding characters.

 Changing Fonts

Footers

Page footers can be added to the bottom of printed worksheets and charts.

Headers and Footers

Formatting

You can add formatting to cells to control value punctuation, alignment of values and labels, font styles and point sizes, border lines, and background cell patterns. You can also add a special type of formatting, called **cell protection,** that prevents changes to cell contents and that hides cell formulas.

Adding background shading ⁘	**Patterns**
Adding border lines ⁘	**Borders**
Alignment of values and labels in cells ⁘	**Aligning Labels and Values**
Changing font styles and point sizes ⁘	**Fonts**
Formatting date values ⁘	**Date Formats**
Formatting time values ⁘	**Time Formats**
Preventing cell changes and hiding cell formulas ⁘	**Cell Protection**
Using (and reusing) formatting combinations ⁘	**Styles**
Value punctuation, including currency symbols and commas ⁘	**Formatting Numbers**

Formatting Numbers

You can add formatting to **values** in two ways: by including the formatting when you enter the value and by choosing the Format Cells command.

Formatting During Data Entry

Often the easier way is to include the formatting when you enter a value into the cell.

	A	B
1	$12,345.67	
2		

This cell holds the value 12345.67. But because I entered $12,345.67 into the cell, Excel formats the cell so that the displayed value shows a dollar sign and a comma.

Formatting with the Format Cells Command

You can also format numbers in selected cells by choosing the Format Cells command and then selecting the Number tab.

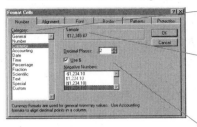

1 Select a formatting category from the Category list box.

2 Look at the Sample field to see how the active cell looks with the selected formatting.

3 Excel displays additional formatting options in the area next to the Category list box. You use these options to further describe the formatting.

 Scientific Notation

Formula Bar   The formula bar is that space under the toolbars.

When you enter **labels**, **values**, and **formulas** into worksheet cells, Excel displays what you enter in the formula bar. If you select a cell by clicking, Excel also uses the formula bar to display the cell's contents. And if you click the formula, Excel lets you edit the cell's contents.

Formulas

In Excel, you use formulas to calculate **values.** To build a formula, select the cell in which the formula should go, type the equals sign (=) to indicate that what you're about to type is a formula, and type the formula using standard arithmetic operators, values, **cell addresses,** and even cell names. If you use a cell address or a cell name, Excel uses the value stored in that cell. I know you did fine in third-grade arithmetic, but just to make sure you understand how all this works, here are some sample formulas:

Formula	What happens
=2+2	Adds 2 and 2, returning the not-surprising result of 4
=24.5-12	Subtracts 12 from 24.5
=I81/U812	Divides the value in cell I81 by the value in cell U812
=RATE*PRINCIPAL	Multiplies the values in the cells named RATE and PRINCIPAL
=1000^2	Squares the value 1000

Excel applies the standard rules of operator precedence in a formula that uses more than one operator: Exponential operations are performed first, then division and multiplication, and then addition and subtraction. But you can override these standard rules by using parentheses. Excel will first perform operations inside parentheses. This probably makes perfect sense to some people, but just to beat this thing to death, here are some more examples of formulas. All use the same values and operators, but they return different results because of the way parentheses change the order of the arithmetic operations.

Formula	Result
=1+2*3	7
= (1+2)*3	9

F

Selective formulas

If you want to count the times a particular value or label occurs in a range of cells, or if you want to tally a value for some subset of the entries in a list (or if you want to do something that sounds like either of these tasks), choose the Data Filter and Data Subtotals commands. Together, they'll make these selective calculations easy and straightforward.

   ❖ **Filtering Lists; Functions; Function Wizard; Subtotaling Lists**

Fractions   To enter a fraction in a cell, type the equals sign and then the fraction. In other words, enter a formula for the fraction. For example, to enter the fraction 1/4, type =1/4. Excel stores the equivalent decimal value for the fraction.

   ❖ **Formulas**

Full Screen   You can use almost all of your screen to display a workbook's sheets. When you view a workbook in a full screen, Excel displays only the menu bar and the workbook. Excel doesn't display the toolbars, the application window's title bar, and the document window's title bar.

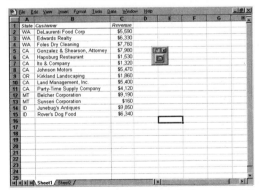

To view the Excel application window as a full screen, choose the View Full Screen command.

To return to the regular view of the application window, choose the View Full Screen command again. Or click the Full Screen button.

Functions

Functions are prefabricated **formulas** you can use to make worksheet construction easier—and more accurate. In a function, you name the formula to be calculated and supply the inputs, or **arguments.**

Conditional test or logical formulas :•* **Conditional Functions**
Date and time value formulas :•* **Date and Time Functions**
Depreciation, investment, and loan formulas :•* **Financial Functions**
Logarithmic, mathematical, trigonometric formulas :•* **Math Functions**
Statistics and database formulas :•* **Statistics Functions**
Table lookup and reference functions formulas :•* **Lookup Functions**
Text string formulas :•* **Text Functions**
Workbook information formulas :•* **Workbook Functions**

Function Wizard

The Function Wizard enters functions into cells, and it also lets you use **functions** to quickly perform complicated calculations.

To use the Function Wizard, follow these steps:

1 Choose the Insert Function command or the Function Wizard tool. Excel displays the first Function Wizard dialog box.

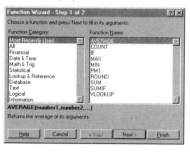

2 In the Function Category list box, select the general type of calculation you want. Excel displays a list of the functions in that category.

3 From the Function Name list, select the calculation you want.

4 Click Next to move to the second Function Wizard dialog box.

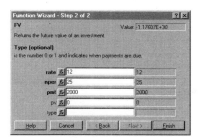

5   Using the text boxes, enter the function arguments as values, cell addresses, or cell names. Excel displays the function value to the right of the text box. (Required argument names appear in **bold**; optional argument names don't.)

6   To use another function's result as an argument, click the Function Wizard button, just to the left of the argument's text box.

7   To place the function into the active cell, click Finish. That closes the Function Wizard dialog box. Then press Enter to move the function to the cell. (If you don't want to place the function into the active cell, click Cancel.)

Formulas

Goal Seek   The Tools Goal Seek command calculates the **formula** input value that causes the formula to return a specified result. You use Goal Seek when you know what formula result you want but don't know what input value returns that result. To illustrate how the Goal Seek command works, suppose you want to know what initial deposit, or present value, results in a future value formula of $500,000 if the annual interest rate is 10 percent and the term is 25 years.

To use Goal Seek, follow these steps:

1   Build a worksheet that includes the future value formula and that uses cell addresses as inputs. In the example, you want to find the initial deposit amount that causes the future value formula in cell B4,=FV(B2,B3,G-B1), to return $500,000.

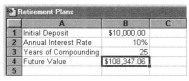

	A	B	C
1	Initial Deposit	$10,000.00	
2	Annual Interest Rate	10%	
3	Years of Compounding	25	
4	Future Value	$108,347.06	
5			

continues

79

G

Goal Seek *(continued)*

2 Choose the Tools Goal Seek command.

3 Enter the cell address with the formula in the Set Cell text box.

4 Enter the target value you want the formula to return in the To Value text box.

5 Enter the cell address with the input value that the Goal Seek command should adjust in the By Changing Cell text box.

Once you've described the Goal Seek operation, Excel begins adjusting the input value, looking for the value that causes the formula to return the target value. If Goal Seek can find an input value that returns the target value, it displays a message box telling you so and then adjusts the input value cell.

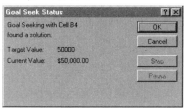

Go To You can quickly move the **cell selector** to another location by using the Name box or the Edit Go To command.

Using the Go To Drop-Down List Box

To quickly move the cell selector to a particular cell, activate the Name box.

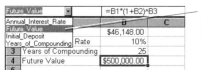

Type the cell address or select a cell name, and then press Enter.

Using the Go To Command

You can also use the Edit Go To command to quickly move to a cell.

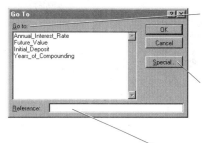

Excel lists any cell names you've defined in the Go To list box. Double-click on any of these to move the cell selector.

Click the Special button if you want to move the cell selector by using cell contents and characteristics. Excel displays the Go To Special dialog box.

In the Reference text box, enter the address of the cell to which you want to move.

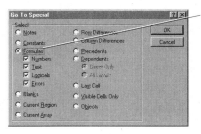

Use the Go To Special dialog box's radio buttons to indicate to what kind of cell the selector should be moved. Marking the Formulas radio button, for example, tells Excel to move the cell selector to the first cell in the selected range with a formula.

Finding Cells

Gridlines Gridlines are the intersecting horizontal and vertical lines that appear on both worksheets and charts.

Gridlines on charts	**Chart Gridlines**
Gridlines on printed worksheets	**Sheet Page Setup**
Worksheet gridlines appearance and color	**Worksheet Views**

Groups A group is a range selection in two or more **worksheets.** You select a group by first making a range selection in the current worksheet and then selecting ranges in additional worksheets. Display additional worksheets by holding down Shift and clicking the worksheet **page tabs.**

You can format groups using the Format Cells command. You can fill groups too, by using the Edit Fill Across Worksheets command.

Filling Cells; Formatting

Headers and Footers Choose the File Page Setup command and select the Header/Footer tab to display a dialog box in which you'll specify how page headers and footers are formatted for printed worksheets and charts.

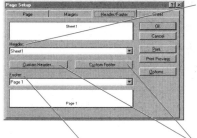

To add a standard header to printed pages, activate the Header drop-down list box and select a header style. Excel provides standard headers that name the sheet, number pages, and identify the author or user.

Use the Custom Header and Customer Footer command buttons to tailor headers or footers to your own needs. Excel displays another dialog box you use to create a header or footer from scratch.

To add a standard footer to printed pages, activate the Footer drop-down list box and select a footer style.

Page header vs. list headers

Unfortunately, Excel uses the term "header" in two ways. One way refers to the page headers Excel sticks at the top of printed pages. The other way refers to the column headings that name the fields used in a list.

 Sheet Page Setup

Help

Need help with some Microsoft Excel task? No problem. Click the Help tool. Excel adds a question mark to the mouse pointer arrow.

To indicate what you want help with, click on the menu command or on a part of a workbook or a window. After you select the item for which you want help, Excel starts the Help application, and Help displays specific information about your selection.

Hiding Formulas Cell Protection

Hiding and Unhiding Sheets

You can hide the active sheet so that it isn't displayed in the workbook window. To do this, choose the Format Sheet Hide command.

To unhide hidden sheets in the selected worksheet group, choose the Format Sheet Unhide command. When Excel displays a list of the hidden sheets in the workbook, click the one you want to unhide. Then click OK.

Groups

Importing Spreadsheet Files
Excel lets you use files created with other spreadsheet programs. To use such a file, choose the File Open command. When Excel displays the Open dialog box, use the List Files of Type drop-down list box to specify which type of file you want to use.

Importing Text Files; Opening Workbooks

Importing Text Files
Excel converts text files—for example, files created with a word processor—for use in an Excel workbook. To convert a text file, take the following steps:

1 Choose the File Open command to retrieve the file. Once you do this, Excel starts the Text Import Wizard.

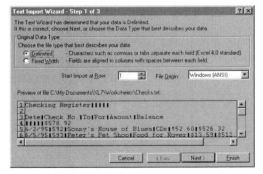

2 Mark the Delimited radio button if the fields, or chunks, of information are delimited. ("Delimited" means that the fields are separated with a character such as a Tab space.)

3 Mark the Fixed Width radio button if the fields of information are arranged neatly into fixed-width columns. (A report that tabulates data would almost always be arranged this way, for example.)

4 Tell Excel which is the first line, or row, you want imported.

5 Specify the operating environment in which the file was created: Windows, Macintosh, MS-DOS, or OS/2. Excel displays the tentative organization of the converted text file at the bottom of the dialog box.

6 Click Next.

7 If you are converting a delimited text file, you use the wizard's second dialog box to identify the delimiter—the character used to separate the chunks of information on a line. If necessary, use the Treat Consecutive Delimiters As One check box and the Text Qualifier drop-down list box to adjust for any conversion problems. (A "text qualifier" is the character used by the **delimited file** to show the beginning and end of text labels.)

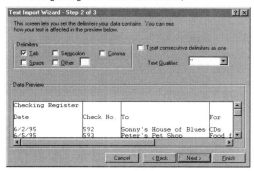

8 If you are converting a nondelimited file, click the mouse to show column borders. Excel adds a vertical arrow to show the border, or break, line. As necessary, remove border lines by double-clicking. As necessary, move border lines by dragging.

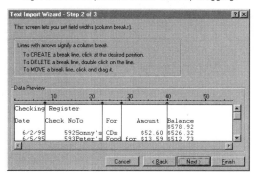

9 Use the Data Preview area to verify the converted data.

10 Click Next when you've described how to convert the delimited or nondelimited file.

continues

Importing Text Files *(continued)*

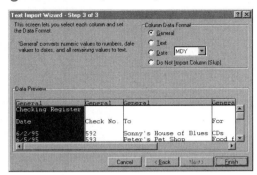

11 Select a column and then a format radio button.

12 Mark the Do Not Import Column (Skip) radio button if you don't want the text file field in the new Excel workbook.

13 Choose Finish to display the converted text file in an Excel workbook. (Once you get the converted text file in an Excel workbook, you'll want to adjust column widths. Be sure also to save the new workbook with the converted text file data.)

For your information

All database and most accounting applications create delimited text files for easy importing into programs such as Microsoft Excel.

Columns; Saving Workbooks

Inserting You can add—or insert—cells, charts, columns, functions, macros, names, notes, page breaks, pictures, objects, rows, and worksheets.

Adding cell notes	**Notes**
Adding cells	**Inserting Cells**
Adding charts	**ChartWizard**
Adding columns	**Inserting Columns**
Adding functions	**Function Wizard**
Adding macros	**Macro**
Adding names	**Names**

Formula adjustments

Excel adjusts formulas when you insert cells, columns, rows, and worksheets.

Inserting Cells
You can insert single cells or groups of cells into rows and columns.

Inserting a Single Cell

Select the cell that occupies the position you want for the new, inserted cell, and then choose the Insert Cells command and complete the Insert dialog box.

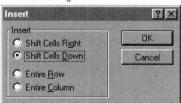

Use the Insert radio buttons to indicate how Excel should make room for the new cell or cells: by moving down the cells in the selected column (indicated as Shift Cells Down) or by moving right the cells in the selected row (indicated as Shift Cells Right).

Don't use the Entire Row or Entire Column radio buttons unless you want to insert a new row above the active cell or a new column left of the active cell.

Inserting Several Cells

Select a range of cells so that the top-selected or left-selected cell occupies the position you want for the top or left new, inserted cell; then choose the Insert Cells command and complete the Insert dialog box. (Excel inserts as many cells as you select.)

❖ **Inserting Columns; Inserting Rows**

Inserting Columns
You can insert single columns or groups of columns into a worksheet.

Inserting a Single Column
Select the column that occupies the position you want for the new, inserted column; then choose the Insert Columns command.

Inserting Several Columns
Select a range of columns so that the leftmost selected column occupies the position you want for the leftmost inserted column; then choose the Insert Columns command. (Excel inserts as many columns as you have selected.)

 Inserting Cells

Inserting Rows
Just as you can insert one or more columns in a worksheet, you can also insert one or more rows.

Inserting a Single Row
Select the row that occupies the position you want for the new, inserted row; then choose the Insert Rows command.

Inserting Several Rows
Select a range of rows so that the topmost selected row occupies the position you want for the topmost inserted row; then choose the Insert Rows command. Excel inserts as many rows as you have selected.

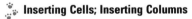 **Inserting Cells; Inserting Columns**

Inserting Worksheets
You can insert as many worksheets as you like in workbooks.

Inserting a Single Worksheet
Select the sheet that occupies the position you want for the new, inserted worksheet; then choose the Insert Worksheets command.

Inserting Several Worksheets

Select a range of worksheets so that the first selected worksheet occupies the position you want for the first inserted worksheet; then choose the Insert Worksheets command. (Excel inserts as many worksheets as you have selected.)

Inserting Cells

Italic Characters

I

You can *italicize* characters in the current worksheet selection by pressing Ctrl+I or by clicking the Italic tool. You can also use the Format Cells command and its Font tab options.

Changing Fonts

Labels

A label is something you enter into a cell but that you don't want to use later in a formula. Usually, a label is a chunk of text or a chunk of text and numbers. But a label might use numbers and still not be something you later want to use in a formula. For example, a telephone number uses numbers, but you probably wouldn't ever use a telephone number in a formula.

Entering Data; Values

List Management

Excel provides a simple database management feature called List Management. You can sort lists, filter them, and subtotal list entries. And you can create PivotTables based on lists.

Analyzing lists	**PivotTables**
Arranging and organizing lists	**Sorting Lists**
Building lists	**Creating Lists**
Creating a new list using a list	**Filtering Lists**
Editing entries in a list	**Editing Lists**
Finding a list entry	**Searching Lists**
Removing, or deleting, entries from a list	**Editing Lists**

Lookup Functions

Lookup functions return specified values or labels from tables or arrays. For example, the following function returns the second label—which is CA—in the array of labels included as arguments:

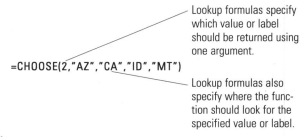

Lookup formulas specify which value or label should be returned using one argument.

=CHOOSE(2,"AZ","CA","ID","MT")

Lookup formulas also specify where the function should look for the specified value or label.

Argument; Function Wizard

Lotus 1-2-3

Lotus 1-2-3 is another spreadsheet program—as you undoubtedly know. What you may not know is that you can open and save Lotus 1-2-3 worksheet files with Microsoft Excel. To do this, you use the Open and Save dialog boxes' List Files of Type list box to specify a Lotus 1-2-3 file format.

Importing Spreadsheet Files; Opening Workbooks; Saving Workbooks

Macro

A macro is simply a series of commands. This doesn't sound very exciting, of course. And maybe it isn't. But you can store macros in separate workbook sheets called, cleverly enough, macro sheets. And you can repeat them, or play them back. With this play-back ability, you can use macros to automate operations that work the same way every time you use them.

Visual Basic

Margins   Choose the File Page Setup command and select the Margins tab to display a dialog box in which you can specify page margins for printed worksheets and charts.

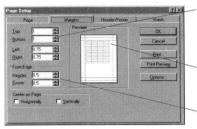

Use the Top, Bottom, Left, and Right boxes to specify the margins in inches.

Look at the Preview box to see the effect of your specifications.

Use the Header and Footer boxes to specify how many inches a header and footer should be from the edge of the page.

 Headers and Footers; Printing

Math Functions   Excel's rich set of arithmetic, logarithmic, and trigonometric functions make for quick mathematical **formulas.** Here's a sampling of what they can do:

Function	What it does
=COS(.5)	Returns the cosine of 0.5, which is 0.877582562
=LOG10(100)	Returns the common logarithm of 100, which is 2
=SQRT(9)	Returns the square root of 9, which is 3

 **Argument; AutoSum; Function Wizard**

Microsoft Query   Microsoft Query is the name of another application, or program, that comes with Excel. I'm not going to describe here how Query works. But I do want you to know that it lets you query external databases, such as those created in Microsoft Access.

Microsoft Word   You can use Microsoft Excel worksheets and charts in your Word documents.

Using Excel Worksheets and Charts with Word

Select the worksheet range or chart and choose the Edit Copy command. Switch to Word, position the insertion point where you want the worksheet or chart, and choose the Edit Paste command.

⁙ **OLE; Switching Tasks**

Moving and Copying Sheets   You can reshuffle the sheets in a workbook by moving (and copying) them. To move a sheet, follow these steps:

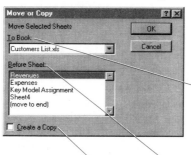

1 Activate the sheet, for example, by clicking on its tab.

2 Choose the Edit Move or Copy Sheet command.

3 Use the To Book drop-down list box to name the workbook to which you want to copy or move the sheet. (The workbook must be open.)

4 Use the Before Sheet list box to indicate in front of which sheet you want to copy or move the sheet.

5 Mark the Create a Copy check box to copy, or duplicate, the sheet rather than move it.

⁙ **Chart Sheets; Worksheets**

Moving Data
You can move data—**values, labels, formulas,** and worksheet ranges—with either the mouse or the Edit Cut and Edit Paste commands.

Moving Data with the Mouse
To move data with the mouse, select what you want to move, then click on the selection border, and then drag the selection.

Moving Data with Edit Cut and Edit Paste
To move data with the Edit Cut and Edit Paste commands, follow these steps:

1 Select the cell or worksheet range you want to move.

 2 Choose the Edit Cut command or the Cut tool.

3 Select the cell to which the copied cell should be moved, or select the cell to which the upper left corner cell of the worksheet range should be moved.

 4 Choose the Edit Paste command or the Paste tool.

Moving formulas

When you move a formula, Excel doesn't adjust relative **cell references** in it.

 Copying Data; Copying Formulas

Moving Objects and Pictures
You can move objects and pictures with the mouse or with commands.

Moving with the Mouse
Simply select the object or picture and then drag it to where you want it.

Excel adds selection handles to the object or picture to show you've selected it. The selection handles are the little black squares that appear at the corners and along each edge.

continues

Moving Objects and Pictures *(continued)*

Moving with Commands

You can also move a graphic object or picture by using the Edit Cut and Edit Paste commands in the same way you move other types of worksheet data.

∴ **Copying Objects and Pictures; Resizing Pictures; Worksheet Pictures**

Names You can name a cell or a range of cells and then refer to that name in **formulas** and in command **dialog boxes.** To name a cell, follow these steps:

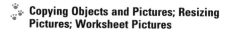
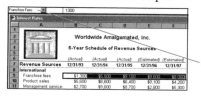

1 Select the cell or range of cells.

2 Click the Name box.

3 Enter the cell or range name into the Name box.

∴ **Formula Bar**

Naming Sheets Excel provides default names for **worksheets** and **chart sheets**—Sheet1, Sheet2, Chart1, and so on—but these names aren't very descriptive.

You can use sheet names to organize your workbooks. To replace Excel's default names, double-click the sheet tab or choose the Format Sheet Rename command.

In the Rename Sheet dialog box, replace the existing sheet name by typing over it.

New Workbooks

To create a new workbook, choose the File New command or click the New Workbook tool. Not very difficult, eh?

Opening Workbooks; Saving Workbooks; Workbooks

Notes

You can use cell notes to document or describe the contents of a cell.

Adding and Editing Notes

To enter or edit a cell note, follow these steps:

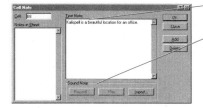

1 Select the cell.

2 Choose the Insert Note command.

3 In the Text Note area, type your note.

4 Get really wacky. You can even add sounds to the cell by using the Sound Note command buttons. (To do this, use the Import command to tell Excel which WAV audio file holds the sound note.)

Locating Notes

To see a cell note, click the cell.

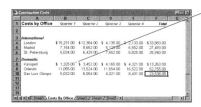

To show you which cells have notes, Excel places a marker in the cell's upper right corner. I removed the **gridlines** on this worksheet to make the note indicator more visible.

OLE

OLE (pronounced "oh-lay") is a Microsoft enhancement to the Windows operating system.

You use OLE to create what's called a "compound document"—a document file that combines two or more types of information. For example, you might want to create a compound document that includes a long report written in, for example, Microsoft Word or WordPerfect. On page 27 of your report, however, you might want to include a worksheet (or worksheet fragment) created in Excel. And perhaps on page 37 of your report, you might want to include a chart created in Excel. So your compound document really consists of stuff created in different applications and pasted together into one big compound document.

Using OLE to Create Compound Documents

To do all this pasting together and combining, you can often use the application's Edit Copy and Edit Paste (or Edit Paste Special) commands. And if you're creating the compound document in Excel, you can use the Insert Object command.

Distinguishing Between Linked Objects and Embedded Objects

A linked object—remember this might be the Excel worksheet you've pasted into a word-processing document—gets updated whenever the source document changes. An embedded object doesn't. (You can, however, double-click on an embedded object to open the application that created the embedded object to make your changes.)

Let me also make what may be an obvious point. If you embed, or copy, stuff into a compound document, it gets bigger. When you simply link stuff, the compound document doesn't really get bigger.

What you absolutely need to know about OLE

Perhaps the most important tidbit for you to know about OLE is that it's very easy to use. You don't have to do anything other than copy and paste the things—called "objects"—you want to plop into the compound document.

 Embedding and Linking Existing Objects; Embedding New Objects

O

Opening Workbooks
To open a previously saved workbook, choose the File Open command. Or click the Open tool. Either way, Excel displays the Open dialog box, shown below.

1 Use the Look In boxes to specify where the workbook file was saved.

2 Use the Files of Type list box if you want to open a file with a format other than that of the usual Excel workbook file. (You might do this if you want to import another spreadsheet program's file.)

3 Use the File Name text box to identify the file.

4 Click the Find Now button to select a file like the one you've described in steps 1,2, and 3.

5 Click OK.

Protecting the original workbook
If you don't want to overwrite the original workbook file, mark the Read Only check box. If you mark this check box and later want to save the workbook, you'll need to use a new file name.

Default Workbooks; File Properties; Saving Workbooks; Troubleshooting: You Can't Find a Workbook

Outlining
Excel has an outlining feature that lets you work with a worksheet as an outline—just as most word processors let you work with documents as outlines. This outlining feature is neat. And I'm sure lots of people use it. But I also think that any time your workbooks become so complicated that you need to outline them, the easier and safer tack is just to simplify the workbook's structure.

Page Breaks
Excel breaks worksheets into page-size chunks automatically as it prints. You can let Excel determine these page breaks, or you can choose where these page breaks occur.

Adding Vertical Page Breaks
Select the column just right of where the worksheet should be vertically split into separate pages, and then choose the Insert Page Break command.

Adding Horizontal Page Breaks
Select the row just below where the worksheet should be horizontally split into separate pages, and then choose the Insert Page Break command.

Removing Page Breaks
Select the column just right of or the row just below the page break, and then choose the Insert Remove Page Break command.

Excel draws a dashed line wherever page breaks occur.

 Printing

Page Numbers
You add page numbers to printed worksheets and charts by adding a header or a footer that includes a page number. You can specify which number Excel uses for the first page. For example, the first page of a printed worksheet shouldn't be numbered 1 if it's the 26th page in a report; it should be numbered 26.

Headers and Footers; Printed Pages Setup

Page Setup

Choose the File Page Setup command and its tab options—Page, Margins, Header/Footer, Sheet, and Chart—to control the appearance of printed worksheets and charts.

Chart appearance ⁙	**Chart Page Setup**
Page appearance ⁙	**Printed Pages Setup**
Page headers and page footers ⁙	**Headers and Footers**
Page margins ⁙	**Margins**
Sheet appearance ⁙	**Sheet Page Setup**

Page Tab

Excel uses page tabs in several ways. One use is to label the workbook sheet. (You can also click sheet page tabs to move through a workbook.) Another use of page tabs appears in some dialog boxes. If a dialog box shows more than will fit within its border, the dialog box includes tabs for going to other pages. On each page is a set of needed input information.

You can move through these pages by clicking on the page tabs. To see an example of how this works, choose the File Page Setup command and then click on the page tabs—Page, Margins, Header/Footer, and Sheet. I'm not going to include a figure that shows this. I don't want to ruin the surprise for you.

⁙ **Naming Sheets**

Pagination

Pagination refers to the process of breaking a document into page-size chunks. You can let Excel paginate your documents. You do this simply by printing the workbook or by print-previewing the workbook. Or you can do it yourself using hard page breaks. You do this with the Insert Page Breaks command.

⁙ **Page Breaks; Printing; Print Preview**

Passwords You can use passwords to limit access to workbooks, to limit changes to workbook files, and to limit changes to cell contents.

| Controlling access to workbook files ⁝ **Save Options** |
| Protecting cells in a workbook ⁝ **Cell Protection** |

Patterns To add background patterns to cells, choose the Format Cells command and the Patterns tab.

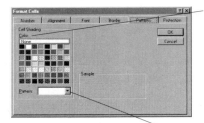

Select the foreground color for the pattern using the colored Cell Shading buttons.

Activate the Pattern list box to choose a pattern and a color for the lines, dots, or cross-hatching that create the pattern.

⁝ **Coloring Worksheet Ranges**

Percentages Percentages are decimal values such as 0.75 formatted as 75%. To store percentages in cells, you can enter them as decimal values and then format them, or you can enter them as percentages. (In this case, Excel stores the decimal value in the cell but formats the decimal value as a percentage.)

⁝ **Entering Data; Formatting Numbers; Fractions**

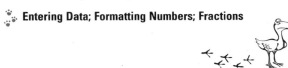

Picture Charts

A picture chart uses little pictures in place of standard chart **data markers** such as pie slices, bars, and lines. You can replace the standard data markers Excel uses for charts with clip art images. To create a picture chart, follow these steps:

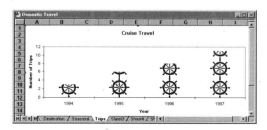

1 Plot your data in a bar, column, or line chart.

2 Copy the picture you want to use in place of the standard data marker to the Clipboard. (You can do this by inserting a picture in an Excel workbook, selecting the picture, and then choosing Edit Copy.)

3 Display the chart.

4 Select the data markers you want to replace by clicking them.

5 Choose Edit Paste.

Clip Art; Clipboard; Worksheet Pictures

PivotTables

PivotTables organize list entries in ways that make the information easier to analyze and understand.

	A	B	C
1	State	Customer	Revenue
2	WA	DeLaurenti Food Corp	$5,590
3	WA	Edwards Realty	$6,330
4	WA	Foles Dry Cleaning	$7,760
5	CA	Gonzalez & Shearson, Attorney	$7,980
6	CA	Hapsburg Restaurant	$1,530
7	CA	Ito & Company	$1,320
8	CA	Johnson Motors	$5,470
9	OR	Kirkland Landscaping	$1,860
10	CA	Land Management, Inc.	$5,400
11	CA	Party-Time Supply Company	$4,120
12	MT	Belcher Corporation	$9,190
13	MT	Sunseri Corporation	$160
14	ID	Junebug's Antiques	$9,850
15	ID	Rover's Dog Food	$6,340

You create PivotTables for lists such as this. The PivotTable in this example could give the number of customers in each state and the sum of revenue for those customers.

continues

PivotTables *(continued)*

To create a PivotTable for a list, follow these steps:

1 Select the list (including the column headings, or headers).

2 Choose the Data PivotTable command. Excel starts the PivotTable Wizard.

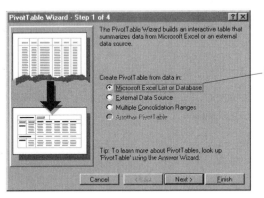

3 Indicate the source you'll use for creating the PivotTable. Usually, you'll use a list, so you mark the first radio button. You can use an external data source, another PivotTable, or a consolidated range. Click Next.

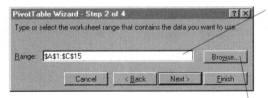

4 Confirm the data source and then click Next. If you use a list, for example, the second PivotTable Wizard dialog box asks for the worksheet range holding the list. (The appearance of the second PivotTable Wizard dialog box depends on the data source used for the PivotTable.)

5 Optionally, click Browse to display a dialog box you can use to open another workbook file—if that's where the list is.

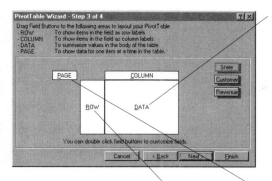

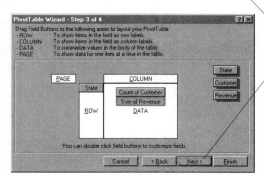

6 Drag the button for the list field you want to summarize to the DATA block. By default, the PivotTable Wizard assumes you want to sum values and count labels. But double-click the button to display a dialog box you can use to select another summary calculation.

7 To arrange list infor-mation on separate worksheet pages or in separate columns, drag buttons to the PAGE or COLUMN blocks.

8 Drag the button for the list field that should show in rows to the ROW block.

9 Click Next when you've described how the PivotTable should look.

10 Use the PivotTable Starting Cell text box to specify the upper left corner of the work-sheet range where you want the PivotTable placed—such as A1 of a new worksheet.

continues

P

PivotTables *(continued)*

11 Use the PivotTable Name text box to name or describe the PivotTable. A Pivot-Table that summarizes client revenue by state, for example, might be named "Customers by State."

12 Use PivotTable Options check boxes to indicate where grand totals should be calculated, whether the PivotTable data should be saved, and whether Excel should Auto-Format the table.

	A	B	C
1	State	Data	Total
2	CA	Count of Customer	6
3		Sum of Revenue	25820
4	ID	Count of Customer	2
5		Sum of Revenue	16190
6	MT	Count of Customer	2
7		Sum of Revenue	9350
8	OR	Count of Customer	1
9		Sum of Revenue	1860
10	WA	Count of Customer	3
11		Sum of Revenue	19680
12	Total Count of Customer		14
13	Total Sum of Revenue		72900

13 Click Finish. Excel creates a PivotTable that summarizes the list information in a table.

Changing PivotTable Organization

You can change the organization of a PivotTable by dragging the list field buttons; drag the State button to the Data button, for example, and Excel flip-flops the PivotTable.

	A	B	C
1	Data	State	Total
2	Count of Customer	CA	6
3		ID	2
4		MT	2
5		OR	1
6		WA	3
7	Sum of Revenue	CA	25820
8		ID	16190
9		MT	9350
10		OR	1860
11		WA	19680
12	Total Count of Customer		14
13	Total Sum of Revenue		72900

Creating Lists

Points

One point equals 1/72 inch. In Excel, you specify font size and row height in points.

Of row heights and font sizes

Funny thing, but a 12-point font won't fit in a row measuring 12 points in height. For this reason, your row height point-size setting needs to exceed your font point-size setting.

Fonts; Rows

Precedents

Precedents are cells that supply other cells' formulas with values. For example, if the formula in cell A1 references cells B12 and E6, the values in cells B12 and E6 must be supplied before the formula in A1 calculates. Cells B12 and E6, then, are precedent cells for A1.

Auditing Worksheets; Dependents

Printed Pages Setup

Choose the File Page Setup command and select the Page tab to display the dialog box you use to specify how pages should print.

1 Use the Orientation radio buttons to specify whether pages should be printed portrait or landscape.

2 Use the Scaling radio button and box to change the size of the printed worksheet or chart by a set percentage.

3 Use the Paper Size and Print Quality drop-down list boxes to choose a different paper size (assuming your printer supports this) and to change the print quality.

4 Tell Excel the page number to assign to the first printed page by using the First Page Number text box.

Printing

 To print the worksheet or chart displayed in a workbook window, choose the File Print command or click the Print tool.

If you choose the File Print command, Excel displays the Print dialog box. Use it to control how Excel prints the worksheet or chart.

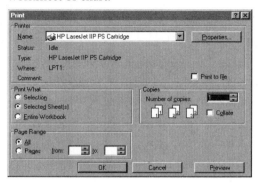

1 Use the Print What radio buttons to indicate whether you want to print the Selection (just the currently selected worksheet range), the Selected Sheets (the sheet that shows plus any others you've selected by pressing Ctrl or Shift and clicking), or the Entire Workbook (all the worksheets and charts in the workbook).

2 Use the Page Range radio buttons and boxes to indicate whether Excel should print all the pages you've indicated by your Print What setting (the usual case) or only a range of pages indicated by your Print What setting.

3 Click OK to print the worksheet.

 Printed Pages Setup; Print Preview

Print Preview

 Choose the File Print Preview command or click the Print Preview tool when you want to see how a workbook's pages will look before you print them. When you choose the command, Excel displays the Print Preview window.

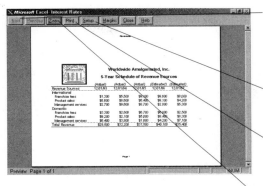

Use the Next and Previous buttons to page back and forth through the printed workbook pages.

Click the Setup button to display the Page Setup dialog box.

Click the Print button to print the workbook. But you probably figured this out yourself, right?

Use the Zoom button to enlarge or reduce the printed page size.

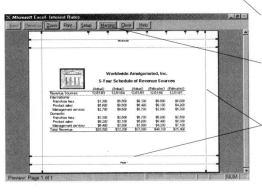

Click the Margins button to tell Excel to display **margin** lines on the Print Preview window's pages.

You can change the page margins by dragging these margin lines.

Printed Pages Setup; Printing

Quattro Pro   Quattro Pro is a spreadsheet program. You can move worksheets between Quattro Pro and Microsoft Excel. Simply specify a Lotus 1-2-3 file format—both Quattro Pro and Excel understand the 1-2-3 file format—when you save and open the worksheets you want to move.

Importing Spreadsheet Files; Opening Workbooks; Saving Workbooks

Range Address

A range address identifies the cells included in a rectangular chunk of a worksheet. A range address consists of the upper left and lower right corner cell addresses, separated by a colon.

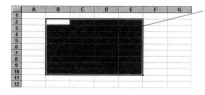

The selected range's address is B2:E10.

Lotus 1-2-3 and range addresses

If you've looked up this entry because you're a Lotus 1-2-3 user and you're having trouble specifying range addresses in Excel, let me make an observation. Your problem—if you want to call it that—probably isn't that you can't figure out how to type some range address such as B2:E10. Your problem is that, in Excel, you need to select the range before you choose commands rather than after you choose them. For example, to erase the contents of the range B2:E10 in Excel, you select the range and then choose the Edit Clear command. In comparison, in Lotus 1-2-3, you would first choose the command Range Erase and then specify the range B2..E10. I hope that helps.

Relative Cell Address

A relative cell address is a **cell address** that Excel adjusts if it's part of a copied formula. OK. That sounds complicated, but here's an example.

	A	B
1	10000	
2	10500	
3	11025	
4		

Say that cell A2 holds the formula =A1*1.05. Excel assumes the cell address in the formula, A1, is relative to the formula location in cell A2.

If you copy the formula from cell A2 to cell A3, Excel adjusts the formula to read =A2*1.05. Because you've moved the formula down one row, Excel moves all the formula cell addresses down one row, too.

 Absolute Cell Address; Copying Formulas; Formulas

Removing Styles To remove, or delete, a **style,** follow these
steps:

1 Choose the Format Style command. Excel, instantly knowing what you're up to, displays the Style dialog box.

2 Select the style from the Style Name box.

3 Click Delete.

 Adding Styles

Repeat You can usually repeat your last change to a workbook
by choosing the Edit Repeat command or by clicking the
Repeat tool.

Undo

Replacing Cell Contents Choose the Edit Replace command to locate cells with specified contents—a fragment
of text, part of a formula, a cell name, a cell address, or a
value—and then replace these contents. To use the Edit
Replace command, follow these steps:

1 Select the worksheet range Excel should search.

2 Choose the Edit Replace command.

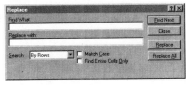

3 In the Find What text box, specify what you want to replace.

4 In the Replace With text box, specify the replacement content.

5 In the Search drop-down list box, indicate whether Excel should search column by column or row by row.

6 Use the Match Case and Find Entire Cells Only check boxes to indicate whether Excel should consider case (lower vs. upper) in its search and look for entire cells rather than parts of cells.

7 Click Find Next to start and restart the search.

8 Click Replace to substitute the replacement text in the active cell.

9 Click Replace All to substitute the replacement text in all cells in the selected area.

Finding Cells

Reports

A report describes the worksheet or worksheet ranges you want to print. If you've created views and scenarios, you can also include different views or scenarios in a report.

To create and use reports, you use the Report Manager. (You install all add-ins, including the Report Manager, by using the Tools Add-Ins command.)

Once you install the add-in, Excel adds the Report Manager command to the View menu. You use it to create and print reports.

Resizing Pictures

Use the mouse to resize drawing objects and pictures. To do this, select the object or picture. Excel marks the object or picture with selection handles. (The selection handles, as you may already know, are those little black squares.) To change the object's or picture's size, drag the selection handles.

Copying Objects and Pictures; Moving Objects and Pictures; Worksheet Pictures

Rows

You can change the height of rows with the mouse or with the Format Row submenu commands. Using the mouse is usually easier. To change the height of a selected row or of several selected rows with the mouse, drag the edge of the row label bottom edge up or down.

	A	B	C
1			
2			
3			
4			
5			

Drag the edge of the row label floor up or down to change a row's height. Excel changes the mouse pointer to a two-directional arrow when you position the mouse pointer on the bottom edge.

Columns

Save Options The File Save As dialog box provides a command button, Options, that lets you protect workbook files from accidental deletion and from people who don't have a **password** to view the workbook. To get to this dialog box, choose the Save As command and then click Options.

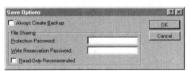

1 Mark the Always Create Backup check box to create a backup copy of the existing, or old, workbook file whenever you save a new copy of the workbook file.

2 You can limit viewing of the file by assigning a protection password. Excel asks for the protection password when someone attempts to open the workbook file using the File Open command.

3 Limit changes to the file by assigning a write reservation password. Excel asks for the write reservation password when someone attempts to open the workbook file. (Even without a write reservation password, someone can still save a copy of the workbook file with a new name.)

4 Mark the Read-Only Recommended check box if you want Excel to display a message that suggests someone open the file with read-only privileges. By opening the workbook file as read-only, you can't save it later except by giving it a new name.

File Properties; Saving Workbooks

Saving Workbooks To save workbooks and the worksheets and charts they contain, you use either the File Save or the File Save As command. Or you can use the Save tool.

Resaving a Workbook

Choose the File Save command when you have saved the workbook before and want to save the workbook using the same name and in the same location. (Or click the Save tool.)

continues

Saving Workbooks *(continued)*

Saving a Workbook for the First Time

 Choose the File Save As command or click the Save tool when you have created a new workbook and haven't yet saved it.

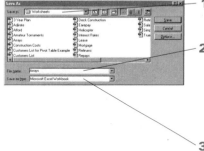

1 Specify where the workbook file should be placed.

2 Name the workbook file, but don't enter the file extension. Excel adds this for you because it uses the file extension to identify the file type.

3 Use the Save As Type list box to save the file in a format other than the usual Excel workbook file format. (Do this, for example, to use the workbook file with another spreadsheet program.)

File Properties; Opening Workbooks; Save Options

Scenarios When you boil it down, a scenario is a collection of values or inputs for specified cells. All you do is store a set of inputs and give the set a name using the Tools Scenarios command. When you want to reuse the inputs, you choose the Tools Scenarios command to indicate which set of inputs you want to use. In effect, then, you get to change as many inputs at once by using a command rather than by having to individually change values in cells.

Scientific Notation
If a cell uses the General number format, Excel uses scientific notation to display values that are too big or too small to fit neatly within the cell's width.

	A	B
1	3E+08	
2	1E-07	
3		

The value 300,000,000 is too big to fit neatly into the standard-width cell, so Excel displays this value as 3E+08, which is equivalent to 3×10^8.

The value 0.0000001 is too small to fit neatly into the standard-width cell, so Excel displays this value as 1E-07, which is equivalent to 1×10^{-7}.

If a value is very large or very small, Excel may even store a value in the cell that uses scientific notation. For example, suppose you typed the digit 3 followed by 21 zeroes:

3000000000000000000000

This value is large in the truest sense, right? Excel agrees. So it uses the scientific notation, 3E+21, both for storing and for displaying the value.

Entering values with scientific notation
You can use scientific notation to enter values into cells too. Although Excel uses an uppercase letter E for scientific notation, you can type either an uppercase E or a lowercase e.

 Entering Data; Formatting Numbers

Scrolling
Scrolling simply refers to paging up and down and left and right in a **workbook**. You can use the horizontal and vertical scroll bars to scroll up and down and right and left if you've got a mouse.

continues

Scrolling *(continued)*

You can also scroll with the keyboard. You can use the PageUp and PageDown keys to scroll up and down. And you can use the Tab and Shift+Tab keys to scroll right and left.

Creating nonscrollable columns and rows

If you use columns and rows to label your worksheet contents, you may not want these labeling columns and rows to scroll. You may want them fixed, or unscrollable. You can do this by creating **window panes**.

⁘ **Finding Cells; Go To; Window Panes**

Searching Lists   To search a list, follow these steps:

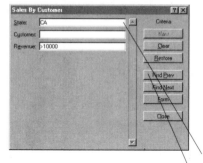

1 Select the list (including the column headings, or headers).

2 Choose the Data Form command.

3 Select the Criteria command button. Excel displays the criteria entry version of the Data Form dialog box.

4 Use the text boxes to describe the list entry you want to find.

5 Use the Find Prev and Find Next command buttons to search backward and forward in a list.

If you enter stuff into the text boxes, Excel looks for an entry that exactly matches what you enter.

You can also search for values based on a conditional, or **Boolean algebra,** test. Here, for example, the criterion >10000 says to find clients providing more than $10,000 of revenue.

All the criteria you enter are used in the search. By entering both a State and a Revenue criterion, as shown here, Excel looks only for California clients providing more than $10,000 of revenue. Note that you don't have to enter the header, or field, name.

When Excel finds a list entry matching your criteria, it displays the list entry in the Data Form dialog box. To continue looking through the list, use the Find Prev and Find Next command buttons. To return to the criteria entry version of the Data Form dialog box—perhaps to specify some new criteria—select the Criteria command button.

Creating Lists; Sorting Lists

Selecting Cells
You select single cells by clicking and dragging or by using the direction keys. (The cell you select is called the **active cell**.)

Selecting a Single Cell

Click on the cell or use the direction keys to move the cell selector to the cell.

Selecting Rectangular Ranges of Cells

You can select more than one cell—what's called a "range"—by dragging the mouse between opposite corners of the range. Or you can select a cell, hold down Shift, and then use the direction keys to select a rectangle of cells. (In a range selection, one cell will still be the active cell.)

Selecting Multiple Ranges of Cells

You can also select discontinuous rectangles of cells by holding down Ctrl and then dragging the mouse between the opposite corners of each range.

Selecting the Worksheet

You can select an entire worksheet by clicking the Select All button, which appears in the upper left corner of the workbook document window.

Selecting Columns
You select a column by clicking on the column letter label. You select a range of columns by clicking on the first column and dragging the mouse to the last column.

Selecting Rows
You select a single row by clicking on the row number label. You select a range of rows by clicking on the first row and dragging the mouse to the last row.

Sharing Microsoft Excel Data
You can easily share **values, labels, formulas,** worksheet ranges, and **charts** created in Excel with other Windows-based applications. To share the data, follow these steps:

1 Select what you want to share: a worksheet range, a chart, some formula fragment, or anything else.

2 Choose the Edit Copy command.

3 Switch to the other application by clicking a Taskbar button.

4 Display the document in which you want to place the Excel information.

5 Paste the contents of the Clipboard into the other application's document. (Probably, you'll do so with that application's Edit Paste command.)

To link or to embed—that is the question
When Windows pastes an object—a worksheet fragment, for example—into another application's document, you'll usually have a choice as to whether the pasted object is linked to the source document or is merely an embedded copy of the source document. Use the Paste Special command to make your choice.

 Clipboard; OLE; Switching Tasks

Sheet Page Setup

Choose the File Page Setup command and mark the Sheet tab to display the dialog box you use to specify how worksheets should appear on printed pages. (The active sheet must display a worksheet for this tab to appear.)

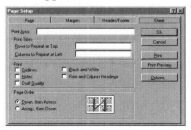

1 Use the Print Area text box to limit the printed portion of the worksheet to a range such as A1:G3. To specify multiple ranges, place commas between the individual ranges, for example, A1:G30, A35:G75.

2 Use the Print Titles text boxes to indicate whether each printed worksheet page should show a column or a row or a set of columns or rows. Do this if you've used rows or columns to hold headings that you want to appear on each page.

3 Use the Print check boxes to indicate whether worksheet gridlines, cell notes, and row numbers and column letters, for example, should print.

4 Use the Page Order radio buttons to indicate the order in which Excel should print the page-size chunks of a worksheet that takes more than a single page to print.

Sheets

Sheets are the pages of a workbook that Excel uses to show **worksheets, chart sheets,** and, in rare circumstances, macro sheets, **Visual Basic** modules, and dialog sheets.

Shortcut Menus

Excel knows which commands make sense in which situations. It also knows which commands you, as an Excel user, are most likely to use. If you want, Excel will display a menu of these commands—called the "shortcut menu." All you need to do is point to whatever you want to fiddle with and click the right button on the mouse.

Solver

Excel provides a Solver add-in that lets you solve optimization modeling problems. You need to specify that you want the Solver when you set up Excel. In an optimization modeling problem, you maximize or minimize an objective function but subject it to constraints. (Once you've installed the Solver add-in, Excel adds the Solver command to the Tools menu.)

.·. **Goal Seek**

Sorting Lists

If you've defined a list using the Data Form command, you can sort the entries alphabetically based on a field that stores labels or in ascending or descending order based on a field that stores a value. To sort a list, follow these steps:

1 Select the list entries.

2 Choose the Data Sort command.

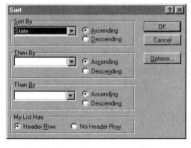

3 Use the Sort By drop-down list box to name the field used for alphabetizing or ordering.

4 Use the Sort By radio buttons to indicate whether you want alphabetic list entries arranged in A to Z or Z to A order or whether you want value list entries arranged in ascending or descending order.

5 Use the Then By drop-down list boxes and radio button sets to add second and third sorting keys.

6 Use the My List Has radio buttons to indicate whether the first selected row names the fields.

The Sort tools

You can use the Sort tools to arrange the selected list entries in either ascending or descending order based on the first field.

.·. **Creating Lists**

Spelling You can use the Tools Spelling command or the Spelling tool to check the spelling of words used in **labels**. To use the command or tool, first select the worksheet area you want to spell-check (if you're interested in checking only a limited area). Then choose the command or tool. Excel displays the Spelling dialog box. Use it to control how Excel spell-checks and what Excel does when it finds a possible error.

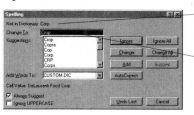

1 Excel alerts you to words it can't find in its dictionary.

2 Excel suggests an alternative spelling with the Change To text box if the Always Suggest check box is marked. You can edit whatever Excel suggests or select another word from the Suggestions list box.

Using the Spelling Command Buttons

Once Excel finds a potentially misspelled word, you use the Spelling command buttons to indicate what Excel should do:

Button	What it does
Ignore	Ignore only this occurrence of the word.
Ignore All	Ignore this and every other occurrence of the word.
Change	Change this occurrence of the word to what the Change To text box shows.
Change All	Change this and every other occurrence of the word to what the Change To text box shows.
Add	Add the word to the spelling dictionary named in the Add Words To combo box.
Suggest	Look through the Excel spelling dictionary and the custom dictionary named in the Add Words To combo box for similarly spelled words.
AutoCorrect	Add the misspelled word and its correct spelling to the list of words and phrases which are corrected automatically.

Starting Excel
You start Excel (and other Windows-based applications) either by opening a document (or file) created by the application or by opening the application itself.

Starting Excel by Opening Documents
To start an application by opening a document, follow these steps:

1 Start Windows Explorer.

2 Display the folder with the document.

3 Double-click the document icon.

Starting an Application Directly
To start an application without opening a document, select the Start button and then the Programs menu. Then, select the application.

About the Documents menu

The Documents menu lists up to 15 of the most recently created documents. If you see the document you want on this menu—remember this may be an Excel workbook—you can open it by selecting it.

Statistics Functions

A statistics function calculates some statistical measure. A special variety of a statistics function—the database functions—even calculates statistical measures of selected values from an Excel list, or database.

Here is a sampling of Excel's general statistics functions:

Function	What it does
=AVERAGE(2,3,4,5,1)	Returns the average of the values 2, 3, 4, 5, and 1, which is 3.
=MAX(23,456,12)	Returns the maximum value included as an argument, which is 456.
=STDEV(2,3,2.5,2,2.5,3)	Returns the sample standard deviation of the values included as arguments, which is 0.447214.

The general statistics functions accept a maximum of 30 **arguments.** Arguments don't have to be values or cell addresses, however. Arguments can also reference worksheet ranges. In this way, you can calculate statistical measurements for large samples and populations. (The worksheet range B1:B10000, for example, is a single argument that references 10,000 cells.)

 **Function Wizard**

Styles

A style is a combination of formatting choices.

Creating a new style  **Adding Styles**	
Deleting an existing style  **Removing Styles**	
Using an existing style  **Applying Styles**	

Subtotaling Lists   Use the Data Subtotals command to subtotal columns with values in a list.

Using the Data Subtotals Command

To use this command, you should first sort the list using the field you'll subtotal. Then select the list (including the column headings, or header row) and choose the Data Subtotals command. Excel displays the Subtotal dialog box.

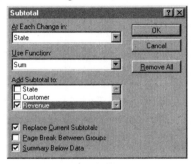

1 Use the At Each Change In drop-down list box to specify where subtotals should be calculated—such as subtotals by state.

2 Use the Use Function drop-down list box to choose which summary calculation Excel should make. (Usually, you sum, but Excel lets you make any statistical calculation: average, maximum, minimum, and so on.)

3 Use the Add Subtotal To drop-down list box to indicate which columns should have subtotals calculated.

4 Use the check boxes to control where Excel places new subtotal information.

5 Click OK. Excel subtotals the list.

Working with Subtotaled Lists

Using the default check box settings, Excel places subtotal and grand total information beneath the list.

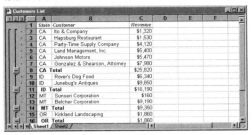

Use the 1, 2, and 3 buttons to tell Excel how much detail it should show in the subtotaled list. The 1 button tells Excel to show only the grand total, 2 tells Excel to show the grand total and any subtotals, and 3 tells Excel to show the individual list entries.

To hide the individual list entries that go into a subtotal, select the minus button. Once Excel hides the list entries that go into a subtotal, it changes the minus button to a plus button. Select the plus button to unhide the list entries.

Subtotaling filtered lists

By subtotaling a filtered list, it's easy to perform many otherwise complicated calculations. Consider, if you will, the possibilities: You can count the times a particular entry occurs by filtering a list so that it includes only the entries you want to count. And you can tally a value field for a subset of list entries. All you need to do is filter the list so that it shows only the subset.

AutoSum; Creating Lists; Sorting Lists

Switching Tasks To multitask, or run multiple applications, in the Windows 95 operating system, you use the Start button and Taskbar. You use the Start button to start new applications. You use the Taskbar to switch, or flip-flop, between the applications you've already started.

This is the Taskbar. The buttons you see represent each of the open applications. To switch to another application, just click its task button.

Tables  **What-If Tables**

Taskbar The Taskbar appears at the very bottom of your screen. It includes the Start button and buttons for any additional **applications** that you or Windows has started. You can use Taskbar's **task buttons** to move another application to the foreground. In many of the figures in this book, I hid the Taskbar. Usually it shows, however.

Switching Tasks

Task Button Windows 95 shows buttons on the Taskbar for each application you or Windows starts. You can make an application the foreground application by clicking its task button.

I don't know what else to call these buttons, so I'm going with "task buttons".

Text Boxes

A text box is a box with text that floats over a worksheet or a chart sheet. Text boxes are, to be honest, the electronic equivalent of car bumper stickers. Even so, you can use them effectively to annotate worksheets and charts.

Adding Text Boxes

To add a text box, follow these steps:

1 Click the Drawing **toolbar's** Text Box tool.

2 Drag the mouse between the initial positions of the upper left and lower right text box corners. Excel draws the text box.

3 Type the text that you want to appear in the box.

> **Save the Whales**

Resizing Text Boxes

Select the text box by clicking on its border; then drag the box's selection handles to change its size.

Moving Text Boxes

Select the text box by clicking on its border; then drag the box to a new location.

Removing Text Boxes

Select the text box by clicking; then press the Del key.

Text Functions

Most functions manipulate values, but Excel also provides functions that manipulate text. The textual arguments in a text function can be either addresses of cells containing text labels or text strings enclosed in quotation marks. Here are some sample text functions:

Function	What it does
=PROPER("mr. president")	Capitalizes initial letter of each word in string, returning Mr. President.
=REPT("Walla",2)	Repeats the first argument the number of times specified in the second argument, returning WallaWalla.
=LEN("Chrysanthemum")	Counts the number of characters in a text string, returning 13.

 **Argument; Function Wizard; Text String Formulas**

Text String Formulas

Excel formulas usually manipulate values arithmetically: adding, subtracting, multiplying, dividing, and exponentiating. (This last word doesn't appear in any dictionary, by the way. I just made it up.) You should know, though, that it's also possible to create formulas that manipulate text by combining text labels, extracting chunks of text from a label, and even changing the capitalization of the letters in a label.

To combine text labels—the simplest text string formula—you use the concatenation operator, &. With the concatenation operator, you can string together two or more pieces of text—including blanks. Here are some examples of text string concatenation formulas. Note that the second and third examples enter a space character between the two words by including a blank character in quotation marks. Note that the third example assumes that cell A1 holds the label Dashiell and that cell A2 holds the label Hammett.

Formula	What it returns
="Walla"&"Walla"	WallaWalla
="Raymond"&" "&"Chandler"	Raymond Chandler
=A1&" "&A2	Dashiell Hammett

For other text string formulas, you'll need to use Excel's **text functions**.

Time Formats

Excel provides time formats that you use to make time decimal values understandable.

Here's a partial list of some of the ways Excel lets you format an example time value, 0.75:

Type	Formatted time value
h:mm AM/PM	6:00 PM
h:mm:ss AM/PM	6:00:00 PM
h:mm	18:00
h:mm:ss	18:00:00
mm:ss	00:00

Formatting Time Decimal Values

To format a time decimal value, follow these steps:

1 Select the cell or range with the time values.

2 Choose the Format Cells command and select the Number tab.

3 Select the Time entry from the Category list box.

4 Choose one of the time format entries from the Type list box.

Note that, near the bottom of the Format Cells dialog box, Excel shows how the active cell looks when formatted with the selected time format code.

 Date Formats; Formatting Numbers; Time Values

Time Functions Date and Time Functions

Time Values Excel lets you use decimal values to represent times: 0 represents 12:00 AM, 0.25 represents 6:00 AM, 0.5 represents 12:00 PM, and so forth. Time values let you easily perform arithmetic using times. For example, you can calculate the number of hours someone works if that person starts at 6:00 AM and works until 3:30 PM.

Date and time combinations

Combine date integer values with time decimal values to show both the date and the time. For example, to represent 12:00 PM on October 28, 1995, you use the value 35000.5. The integer portion of the value, 35000, is the date value for October 28, 1995. The decimal portion of the value, 0.5, is the time value for 12:00 PM.

 Date and Time Functions; Formulas; Time Formats

TipWizard

 You can tell Excel you want pointers while you work. Excel's TipWizard will then provide a list of tips, hints, and pointers related to whatever you're working on.

Displaying the TipWizard's Tip List

To display a list box packed with Excel tips, click the TipWizard tool. Click on the up and down arrows to scroll through the tip list.

Removing the TipWizard's Tip List

When you click the TipWizard tool, Excel depresses the button to show that the TipWizard is busily working away. To remove the TipWizard's tip list, click the TipWizard toolbar button again.

 Help

Toolbars

Toolbars are those rows of buttons and boxes that appear at the top of your window just below the menu bar. Excel initially places the Standard toolbar and the Formatting toolbar in its application window. But Excel also provides several other toolbars.

Adding and Removing Toolbars

You can add and remove any toolbars by pointing to the toolbar, clicking the right mouse button (instead of the usual left button), and then—when Excel displays a list of the available toolbars—selecting the one you want. (You can also use the View Toolbars command to accomplish the same thing.)

Toolbar button names

When you place the mouse just below a toolbar button, Excel displays the button name in a tiny yellow box, called a "ToolTip."

 Quick Reference: Button Guide

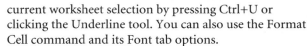

TrueType   TrueType is Microsoft Corporation's scalable font technology. If you're working with Excel, using TrueType fonts in your documents delivers a major benefit. Because of the way a scalable font is created, it's easy for Excel to change, or rescale, the point size in a way that results in legible fonts. Excel identifies TrueType fonts in the various Font list boxes with the **Tr** prefix.

 Changing Fonts; Fonts

Underline Characters   You can underline characters in the current worksheet selection by pressing Ctrl+U or clicking the Underline tool. You can also use the Format Cell command and its Font tab options.

Changing Fonts

Undo   You can usually undo your last change to a workbook by choosing the Edit Undo command or by clicking the Undo tool.

After you choose the Edit Undo command or the Undo tool, Excel changes the command name to Redo. Choose Edit Redo to undo the effect of choosing Undo.

Irreversible damage

The Edit Undo command undoes workbook changes made with the Edit, Insert, and Format menu commands and some changes made with the Data menu commands. The command also undoes workbook changes made by entering or editing data in cells. The Edit Undo command doesn't undo all workbook changes, however. For example, you can't undo workbook changes made with File menu commands.

Values   A value is a number you enter in a cell that you want to later use in a formula. In general, a value can include the numbers 1, 2, 3, 4, 5, 6, 7, 8, 9, and 0 and the period symbol to indicate a decimal point, if needed. You can also include numeric formatting with a value—for example, currency symbols and commas—if you want Excel to use the formatting to display the value. If you want to enter a negative value, precede the number with a hyphen or enclose it in parentheses.

> **Entering Data; Formatting Numbers; Labels; Scientific Notation**

Views   You can tell Excel to remember the way a worksheet appears in the workbook window: its size, position, displayed area, and so on.

Creating a View

You can create a view by choosing the View View Manager command and then clicking the Add button. Microsoft Excel displays the Add View dialog box, which you use to name the view.

Name the view using the Name text box.

Using a View

To see the view, choose the View View Manager command, select the view, and then click the Show button.

W

Visual Basic Visual Basic is Excel's built-in programming language. Visual Basic is way cool. It's also way, way beyond the scope of this book.

 Macro

What-If Tables What-if tables show a series of calculations using the same formula but a different value for each calculation. You might use a What-if table, for example, to forecast the different future value amounts you accumulate in a retirement account based on different annual contributions.

Creating a What-If Table

	A	B
1		$0.00
2	2000	
3	2500	
4	3750	

Leave an input cell at the left corner of the What-if table; Excel needs this for the calculations.

Enter the What-if formula next to the input cell. The formula should reference the empty cell and any other needed inputs. This formula, for example, uses the future value function =FV(0.1,35,-A1).

Enter the input values for the What-if calculations in the column beneath the input cell.

continues

131

What-If Tables *(continued)*

Performing What-If Analysis

Once you've set up the What-if table, follow these steps:

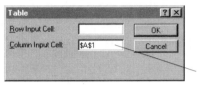

1 Select the What-if table.

2 Choose the Data Table command.

3 Use the Column Input Cell text box to identify the What-if input cell.

4 Click OK.

	A	B
1		$0.00
2	2000	542048.74
3	2500	677560.92
4	3750	1016341.4

Excel uses the What-if formula to calculate results for each of the input values and then places these values in the cells beneath the What-if formula.

The future value amount accumulated based on $2,000 a year contribution, a 10 percent annual return, and 35 years of contributions is $542,048.74.

Table recalculation

Excel uses a special **function**, =TABLE(), to calculate the What-if formula values. If you change an input, Excel recalculates the What-if table value that uses the input. For example, if you want to see the future value amount accumulated based on a $5,000 a year contribution, change the value in cell A4 to 5000.

⁙ Function Wizard; Goal Seek

Window Buttons

Arranged along the outside edge of the application and document windows are buttons. You can use these buttons to display the Control menu, to close windows, and to minimize and change window sizes. The table below shows the way these buttons look for the Excel application window and its document window:

	Displays the Excel application's Control menu. (Different applications use different icons, as you might have guessed. This is the icon for Microsoft Excel.)
	Displays the document window's Control menu.
	Minimizes a window by turning it into a button.
	Restores a window to its previous size.
	Maximizes a window. Maximized application windows fill the screen. Maximized document windows fill the application window.
	Closes the window. Closing an application window, by the way, closes the application.

Window Panes

If you use rows to label columns or columns to label rows, you may want these rows and columns to stay visible—even when you scroll up and down and left and right in a worksheet. To fix the placement of labeling rows and columns, you turn the labeling rows and columns into "panes." Then you freeze the panes.

Creating Window Panes

Position the **cell selector** at the cell below the row and right of the column you want to use as panes. Then choose the Window Split command.

Freezing Window Panes

To freeze—or to simultaneously create and freeze the panes—so that they label columns and rows even as you scroll down and right, choose the Window Freeze Panes command.

Removing Window Panes

To remove a window pane, choose the Window Remove Split command. (This command replaces the Window Split command once you've split a window into panes.)

Unfreezing Worksheet Panes

To unfreeze a window pane, choose the Window Unfreeze Panes command. (This command replaces the Window Freeze Panes command once you've frozen a window's panes.)

Jumping between window panes

You can move the cell selector between window panes by pressing F6.

Workbook Functions

Workbook functions return information about a workbook, your computer, or the operating environment. For example, the following function tells Excel to retrieve information about the operating system:

=INFO("osversion")

If you're using Windows 95, this function returns the string "Windows (32 bit) 4.00."

Argument; Function Wizard

Workbooks Excel arranges **worksheets** and **chart sheets** into stacks of sheets—analogous to a pad of spreadsheet paper. Excel calls these stacked sheets workbooks; and it stores workbooks as files on disk.

> **New Workbooks; Opening Workbooks; Saving Workbooks**

Worksheet Pictures You add pictures to worksheets with the Insert Picture command. When you choose this command, Excel displays the Picture dialog box, which you use to identify the picture file you'll add.

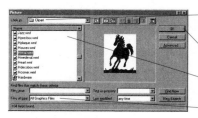

Use the Look In list box to find the picture file.

Click OK to, well, insert the picture.

Use the Name box to identify the picture file.

Use the Files of Type drop-down list box to specify which types of picture, or graphic, files you want to see listed.

A worksheet with a picture.

> **Clip Art; Copying Objects and Pictures; Moving Objects and Pictures; Resizing Pictures**

Worksheets   An Excel workbook consists of worksheets and **chart sheets.** A worksheet is the on-screen spreadsheet. Organized into rows and columns, it lets you easily build tables of labels, values, and formulas.

    Workbooks

Worksheet Titles   Worksheet titles is a Lotus 1-2-3 term. It refers to rows you fix because they label columns and columns you fix because they label rows. (By "fix," I mean you don't want them scrolled when you scroll down and right in the worksheet.) Excel doesn't use worksheet titles. Excel does, however, provide Window panes, which let you accomplish the same thing.

    Window Panes

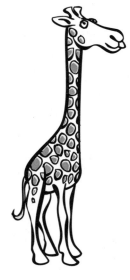

W

Worksheet Views

You can control the appearance of the worksheet. To do so, choose the Tools Options command, select the View tab, and then make your changes.

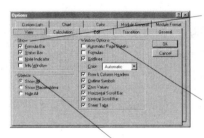

Use the Show check boxes to indicate whether you want the Formula Bar, Status Bar, Note Indicator, and Info Window to appear.

Use the Window Options check boxes to control whether worksheets show, for example, automatic page breaks, formulas (instead of the usual, formula results), and gridlines.

Use the Objects radio buttons to indicate how worksheet objects should appear. Show All displays the object. Show Placeholders tells Excel to display a gray rectangle in place of the object. Hide All hides the object and displays no placeholder.

Workspace

A workspace is a list of workbooks. You can save a workspace, or workbook list, with the File Save Workspace command—in which case you save each of the open workbooks and the list of the open workbooks. To later reopen each of the workbooks listed in the workspace, you open the workspace. Saving a workspace, by the way, works just like saving a workbook.

Save Options; Saving Workbooks

Zooming
You can magnify and reduce, or shrink, the size of the **worksheet** or the **chart sheet** shown on your screen.

Magnifying

`200%`

Activate the Zoom Control tool's drop-down box on the Standard toolbar. Then select a percentage. Selecting 200%, for example, magnifies everything to twice its actual size.

Shrinking

Activate the Zoom Control tool's drop-down list box on the Standard toolbar. Then select a percentage. Selecting 50%, for example, reduces everything to half its actual size.

Actual size may vary

When you zoom a worksheet or a worksheet selection, you don't change the character point size, column widths, or row heights. You simply magnify or shrink the display. As a result, zooming doesn't change what your printed worksheets and charts look like. To do that, you use the Format Cells, Format Rows, and Format Columns commands.

TROUBLE-SHOOTING

Got a problem? Starting on the next page are solutions to the problems that sometimes plague new users of Microsoft Excel. You'll be on your way—and safely out of danger—in no time.

CELL ENTRIES

You Can't Show Long Labels

A label that is longer than a cell is wide won't fit in the cell. Microsoft Excel, however, is not without compassion.

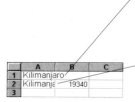

As long as the cell immediately to the right is empty, Excel lets the long label, Kilimanjaro, spill over.

If the neighboring cell contains data, however, the displayed label, Kilimanjaro, is truncated to fit the width of the cell. Although the cell still holds the entire long label, only a portion of the label is displayed.

You can deal with cut-off labels in several ways.

Shorten the label.

You can shorten the label by editing it, for example. (Perhaps all you need to do is abbreviate some word.)

Use smaller characters.

1 Choose the Format Cells command.

2 Select the Font tab option for font and point-size changes.

Increase the column width.

	A	B	C
1	Kilimanjaro		
2	Kilimanjaro	19340	
3			

And this is easy—simply choose the Format Column AutoFit Selection command.

Split the label into separate lines.

	A	B	C
1	Mount Kilimanjaro		
2	Mount Kilimanjaro	19340	
3			

1. Choose the Format Cells command.

2 Select the Alignment tab options and mark the Justify option button so that Excel splits the label into separate lines.

3 Increase the row height (if necessary) by choosing the Format Row Auto Fit command.

💥 Aligning Labels and Values; Columns; Rows

You Can't Show a Value—Except as ######

If a cell isn't wide enough to display a value, Excel shows a series of # symbols. Take a peek, for example, at the worksheet fragment below.

In cell A1, the value 1000000 is too big to fit, so Excel displays a series of # symbols.

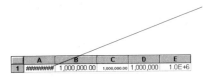

	A	B	C	D	E
1	########	1,000,000.00	1,000,000.00	1,000,000	1.0E+6

In the other cells, though, I've made formatting changes, so the value fits.

continues

You Can't Show a Value... *(continued)*

 Increase the column width.

Choose the Format
Column AutoFit Selection
command.

 Use smaller characters.

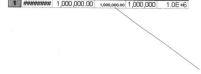

1 Choose the Format
Cells command.

2 Select the Font tab option for font and point-
size changes.

3 Select a condensed
font, if available.

4 Select a smaller point
size, if appropriate.

**Format the number with fewer punctua-
tion characters: commas, currency symbols, decimal places, and so on.**

This is just a matter of selecting a number format that
uses fewer punctuation characters.

If you're using currency symbols and commas, for example, switching to a format that uses only commas
will save a single character, the dollar sign.

If you're working with
two decimal places and
switch to a format with
zero decimal places,
you'll save three
characters: the two
decimal places and the
decimal point.

Use the General number format.

It converts values that are too wide to **scientific nota-tion.** To use the General number format, follow these steps:

1 Select the worksheet range with the cells you want to reformat.

	A	B	C	D	E
1	########	1,000,000.00	1,000,000.00	1,000,000	1.0E+6

2 Choose the Format Cells command.

3 Click the Number tab.

4 Select the General op-tion from the Category box.

 Columns; Formatting Numbers; Rows

You Can't Enter a Label

If you try to enter a **label** that looks like a **value,** Excel may enter what you type as a value—not as a label.

Add a label prefix.

You can force Excel to accept a cell entry as a label, however, by typing an apostrophe and then the label.

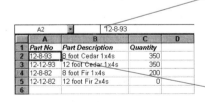

	A2	▼	'12-8-93	
	A	B	C	D
1	Part No	Part Description	Quantity	
2	12-8-93	8 foot Cedar 1x4s	350	
3	12-12-93	12 foot Cedar 1x4s	350	
4	12-8-82	8 foot Fir 1x4s	200	
5	12-12-82	12 foot Fir 2x4s	0	
6				

The apostrophe—which you can barely see here, so look care-fully—tells Excel that this is a label and not a value.

This looks like a value, but really it's a label. If you enter it as a value, by the way, Excel assumes it's a date value.

continues

You Can't Enter a Label *(continued)*

Use the Text function.

If you don't want to include a label prefix, you can also use the **Text function.** Use the **Function Wizard** to build the Text function.

In using the Text function, you'll need to provide the value that you really want entered as a label and a number format, which should be used to format the value before it becomes a label. (If you don't know which number you want, simply specify the General format.)

You Can't Enter Anything into a Cell

If you want to enter something into a cell but Excel won't let you, don't worry. The problem isn't you. Someone told Excel to lock its cells. If the certain someone who did this has, like, half a clue, it probably means you're not supposed to be entering data into the cell.

Unlock the cell protection.

If you're sure you should be entering data into a locked cell, you can unlock, or unprotect, the cell. To do this, choose the Tools Protection Unprotect Sheet command. Excel may prompt you for a password if whoever locked the cells assigned a password. You'll need to give this password to Excel.

 Cell Protection

CALCULATING FORMULAS

You Can't Get a Workbook to Calculate

If you've set a workbook to manual recalculation (or someone in your office has—perhaps without your knowledge), you'll need to tell Excel when it should recalculate workbooks. Fortunately, Excel will tell you whenever it thinks you should consider recalculating.

Ready	Calculate

The Status Bar shows the word Calculate whenever a workbook needs to be recalculated.

Manually force recalculation.

To tell Excel it should recalculate the workbook, you can press F9.

Make worksheet calculation automatic.

To tell Excel it should automatically recalculate a workbook, choose the Tools Options command and then select the Calculation tab.

Mark the Calculation Automatic radio button to tell Excel it should recalculate formulas any time their inputs change.

You can also tell Excel to recalculate the workbook by clicking the Calc Now command button.

Calculating a single cell

You can tell Excel to calculate the formula in a single cell by double-clicking on the cell and then pressing Enter. Note, however, that if the cell's formula depends on the results of other formulas, these other formulas don't get recalculated. They may need to be recalculated, however, if their inputs have changed.

Excel Doesn't Recognize Your Entry as a Formula

If Excel looks at the formula you enter but doesn't think it's a formula, you've forgotten to start the formula with an arithmetic operator such as the equal sign (=).

Edit the formula.
Simply edit the formula so that it starts with an equal sign or a plus sign.

 Formulas

You Can't Correctly Calculate a Formula

If you're just starting out, this can be mighty frustrating. But, rest assured, Excel is calculating the formula correctly. The problem, as painful as it may be to admit, is that the formula you've entered isn't actually the one you want to calculate. In a nutshell, your problem really boils down to one of operator precedence.

Override the standard operator precedence.
To force Excel to calculate in the order you want, enclose the calculation you want made first in parentheses. Then enclose the calculation you want made second in parentheses. Then enclose the calculation you want made third in parentheses, and so on.

 Formulas

A Financial Function Doesn't Work Correctly

Excel's financial functions are extremely powerful, but they're sometimes hard to use. Excel requires the function **arguments** to follow a very specific set of rules. If you can't get a financial function to calculate correctly, your situation most likely boils down to a problem with one of the arguments, as described in the following paragraphs:

Use a decimal interest rate.

The interest argument that most of the financial functions use is a decimal value. The interest rate 8 percent, for example, is actually the decimal value 0.08. One of the more common mistakes new users of Excel make, unfortunately, is entering this decimal value as an integer such as 8. If you enter 8 instead of 0.08, you've actually specified the interest rate as 800 percent and not as 8 percent.

Use a periodic interest rate.

Forgetting to enter an interest rate as a decimal value isn't the only common problem people have with the interest rate argument. Another problem is not using a periodic rate. This almost always boils down to using an annual interest rate in a monthly loan payment formula. But you can't do this. The payment periods—such as months—must agree with the interest rate periods. If you're calculating a monthly loan payment, you need to use a monthly interest rate. If you're calculating the principal balance on a loan with quarterly payments, you need to use a quarterly interest rate. If you're calculating the future value accumulated in a bi-monthly savings plan, you must use a bi-monthly interest rate.

Converting annual interest rates

In almost all cases, you can convert an annual interest rate to a periodic interest rate by dividing the number of periods in a year by the annual interest rate. For example, because there are 12 months in a year, if the annual interest rate is 6 percent, you can calculate the monthly interest rate by dividing 6 percent by 12, for a result of 0.5 percent.

Differentiate cash inflows and outflows with signs.

One other quirky but quite logical aspect of Excel's financial function set is that it requires you to differentiate cash inflows and outflows: Money you pay out needs to be included as a negative value, and money you receive needs to be included as a positive value. You indicate negative argument values with a minus sign.

continues

A Financial Function Doesn't Work Correctly *(continued)*

This sounds complicated, but really it's not. Take the case of a loan payment calculation made with the loan payment function. The dollar amount included as a loan balance amount is a positive amount (because you receive the loan from the lender), and the payment amount, calculated by the function in this case, is a negative value (because you will pay out the loan payment).

Here's another example. Say you will save $2,000 a year and want to estimate the future value you accumulate using the Future Value function. In this case, the $2,000 payment argument is a negative value (because you pay out this amount), and the future value amount returned by the function is a positive amount (because you will receive this amount at some point in the future).

⁙ Financial Functions; Formulas

PRINTING

**You Can't Fit
Something on a
Printed Page
(or Two)**

Let's say you've got something that you want to fit on a single printed page—or even a couple of pages. Unfortunately, the print area is a bit too large. You've got two basic options for dealing with this problem.

Change the worksheet dimensions.

You can make a worksheet smaller by using shorter rows and narrower columns. Use the Format Row command to shorten row heights. Use the Format Column command to narrow columns. Note that you may have problems with labels getting cut off and values getting displayed as a series of # symbols as you shorten and narrow.

Reduce the printed size.

If you don't want to change the physical size of a worksheet but only its printed size, you can tell Excel to fit a worksheet (or set of worksheets) on a specified number of pages.

1 Choose the File Page Setup command and select the Page tab.

2 Mark the Fit To radio button.

3 Use the Fit boxes to indicate how many pages wide by how many tall Excel should print.

4 Select Print. Excel prints the worksheet on the specified number of pages by reducing the worksheet size. With a little luck, you'll still be able to read what Excel prints.

Previewing pages

Remember, to see what your printed pages will look like, choose the File Print Preview command.

 Printing

You Can't Tell Where Excel Breaks Pages

Microsoft Excel automatically breaks a big worksheet into page-size chunks. If you're someone who's not all that fond of surprises, you may want to see where these page breaks will occur before the actual printing.

 Print Preview a workbook.

To get this information, choose the File Print Preview command and then close the Print Preview window.

Once Excel breaks a worksheet into page-size chunks, vertical and horizontal page breaks display as dashed lines.

 Print Preview

You Want to Cancel a Printing Workbook

If you've told Excel to print a workbook that you later realize you don't want to print, you may want to cancel the printing. This is particularly true if the workbook requires many pages to print.

Delete the print job.

When Excel prints a workbook, it creates a print spool file that it sends to Windows 95. Windows 95 then prints this print spool file as well as any other spool files that Excel and other applications have sent. To cancel a printing Excel workbook, therefore, you need to follow these steps:

1 Click the Start button and then choose Settings and Printers to display the Printers window.

2 Double-click the printer icon for the printer you're using to display the print queue for the printer.

3 Click the printing Excel workbook.

4 Press Del or choose the Document Cancel Printing Command.

 Printing; Switching Tasks; Window Buttons

FILES

You Can't Remember Your Password

If you or someone else assigned a read reservation password to a workbook file by using the Save Options command button, you'll need to supply that password before you open the file. If you forget your password or can't seem to enter it correctly, Excel won't let you open the workbook.

Try a password with different-case letters.
Excel differentiates passwords on the basis of the letter-case. The following words, for example, are all different passwords from Excel's point of view: Wathers, wATHERS, and WATHERS. For this reason, if you think you know the password, try changing the lowercase letters to uppercase letters and vice versa. It may be that you entered the password with a different combination of uppercase and lowercase letters than you think. (This can occur, for instance, if you happened to press the Caps Lock key before entering the password.)

 Opening Documents; Saving Documents; Save Options

You Can't Find a File

I love large hard disks. It's great, just great, to have hundreds and hundreds of megabytes of storage. All that room makes it easy to misplace a file, however. Fortunately, Windows 95 provides an extremely powerful tool for finding lost files, the Find File application. Because Excel workbooks are files, you can use the Find File application to locate lost workbooks.

Because the Find File application is so powerful and terribly useful, I'm going to describe it in detail here.

continues

You Can't Find a File *(continued)*

Use the Find File application.

To start the Find File application, click the Start button, and then choose Find, and then Files or Folders. Windows 95 displays the Find: All Files dialog box.

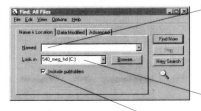

1 If you know the file name, enter it in the Named box. You can use wildcard characters as part of the file name.

2 Tell Windows 95 where to look by using the Look In box.

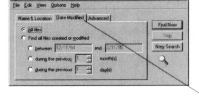

3 Mark the Include Subfolders check box if you want to look in both the folders and subfolders of the disk you identified using the Look in box.

4 Optionally, use the Date Modified tab's options to describe the last modification date of the file you're looking for.

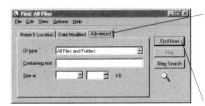

5 Optionally, use the Advanced tab's options to describe either some string of text a file contains or the file size.

6 Click Find Now to start the search for the file or files you've described. When Windows 95 completes its search, it displays the Find: All Files window with a list of the files.

Multitasking is cool

If you describe a sophisticated search—say one that looks for a chunk of text within files—the search can take a long time. Perhaps hours or even days. But this doesn't have to be a problem. You can run other **applications** at the same time. All you need to do is start the other applications.

Switching Tasks

You Accidentally Erased a File

If you erase, or delete, a file and later realize you shouldn't have, all is not lost. As mentioned earlier, the Recycle Bin stores deleted files. Your recently deleted file is probably in the Recycle Bin. (Note that when the Recycle Bin eventually does fill up, Windows 95 makes room for new deleted files in the Recycle Bin by removing the oldest deleted files. So you can't undelete really old files using the Recycle Bin.)

Recycle the file.

To unerase a file you've previously deleted, recycle the file by following these steps:

1 Display the Recycle Bin window by double-clicking the Recycle Bin icon.

2 Select the file you want to unerase.

3 Choose the File Restore command.

WINDOWS AND APPLICATIONS

You Can't Get an Application to Respond

It's unlikely but still possible for a bug in an application to cause it to stop responding, or, in the parlance of computer geeks, "hang." If this happens, you won't be able to choose menu commands within that application. (You would still be able to choose menu commands in other applications, by the way.) And you may not be able to move the mouse pointer or click the mouse. (My experience is that the mouse pointer usually also looks like a hourglass.)

Be patient.

It's possible that the application isn't actually unresponsive. It's possible that it's busy working on something you told it to do. Like saving the document to disk. It's even possible that the application is busy working on something you didn't tell it to do. A spreadsheet application might be busy breaking a long document into pages, for example.

For this reason, the first thing I'd try is a short break. Perhaps coffee and a cinnamon roll. I'm sure, too, that this strategy, which I've adopted as my own first defense, has nothing to do with my growing weight problem. It couldn't.

Terminate the hung application.

Unfortunately, if an application truly is unresponsive—if it ignores your keyboard and mouse actions—there's nothing you can do to make it start responding again. When this is the case, however, you can press Ctrl+Alt+Del. (You'll have to find these three keys on your keyboard first, of course.)

Ctrl+Alt+Del—you press the three keys simultaneously—tells Windows to look at each of the applications you've started, check for responsiveness, and display the Close Application dialog box.

Using the Close Application dialog box, Windows 95 identifies any unresponsive application as "hung." To terminate an application, including one that is hung, select it and then click the End Task command button. To remove the Close Application dialog box, click the Cancel button.

You Get an Application Error

Sometimes an application—even Excel—asks Windows 95 to do the impossible. When this happens, Windows 95 displays a message box that says there's been an accident and that you had better come quick.

Close the application.

When Windows does alert you to an application error, it usually gives you two choices: Close and Details. You want to select Close. Details just gives you the gory specifics of what caused Excel to go toes up.

It's also possible in rare cases for Windows 95 to give you the option of ignoring the error. Even in this case, the most prudent choice is still usually to close the application. But you may like to live dangerously. You may enjoy life on the edge. ("The bleeding? Oh, don't worry. It doesn't look all that bad.")

By the way, if you've been working with some workbook and have made changes you haven't yet saved, and you have the option of ignoring the error, you should ignore the application error and then save the document. Do save the document using a new file name, however. You don't want to replace the previous version of a document with a new corrupted document. Then, once you've saved the document, close the application.

QUICK REFERENCE

Any time you explore some exotic location, you're bound to see flora and fauna you can't identify. To make sure you can identify the commands and toolbar buttons you see in Microsoft Excel, the Quick Reference describes these items in systematic detail.

WORKSHEET MENU GUIDE

File Menu

New...	Opens a new, blank workbook
Open...	Retrieves an existing workbook or workspace from disk
Close	Removes the active workbook's window from the screen
Save	Resaves the active workbook as long as you've already saved it once before
Save As...	Saves a workbook the first time
Save Workspace...	Saves all the open workbooks and also creates a list of open workbooks
Properties	Displays information about the active workbook
Shared Lists...	Lists users working with a notebook and describes what they can and can't do
Page Setup...	Describes the layout of printed workbook pages
Print Area	Displays the Print Area submenu
	Set Print Area Tells Excel to print the selected worksheet range whenever you choose the File Print command
	Clear Print Area Removes the print area specified by the Set Print Area command
Print Preview	Displays a window showing how printed workbook pages will look
Print...	Prints the active workbook
Send...	Sends an Excel workbook to someone else in an e-mail message
Add Routing Slip...	Adds or changes the e-mail routing slip for an Excel workbook
Exit	Closes, or stops, the Microsoft Excel application

Numbered File menu commands

Excel also lists as File menu commands the last four workbooks or workspaces you saved. You can open a listed workbook or workspace by selecting it from the File menu.

Edit Menu

Undo	Reverses, or undoes, the last workbook change
Repeat	Duplicates the last workbook change
Cut	Moves the current workbook selection to the Clipboard
Copy	Moves a copy of the current workbook selection to the Clipboard
Paste	Moves the Clipboard contents to the active workbook
Paste Special...	Moves some portion of the Clipboard contents to the active workbook
Fill	Displays the Fill submenu

Down Copies contents of the selected column's top cell to the rest of the column

Right Copies contents of the selected row's left cell to the rest of the row

Up Directs the gasoline station attendant to top off your car's tank

Left Copies contents of the selected row's right cells to the rest of the row

Across Worksheets... Copies contents of the selected group's first worksheet range to the rest of the group's worksheets

Series... Describes a pattern of values or labels that Excel should use to fill the selected range

Justify Arranges the active cell's text label so that it fits the selected range

Clear	Displays the Clear submenu

All Erases contents, formats, and notes of selected cells

Formats Erases formatting—numeric, alignment, fonts, and so on—of selected cells

continues

Edit Menu *(continued)*

Contents Erases contents—labels, values, or formulas—of selected cells

Notes Erases notes attached to selected cells

Delete... Removes the selected cell, column, or row from worksheet

Delete Sheet Removes selected worksheet from workbook

Move or Copy Sheet... Changes current worksheet's position in workbook or duplicates current worksheet

Find... Looks for cell matching a specified description

Replace... Looks for cell matching specified description and, optionally, replaces its contents

Go To... Moves the cell selector to a specified location

Links... Describes, updates, and changes selected object's link

Object Changes selected object's border, background pattern, and protection

View Menu

Formula Bar Turns off and on the display of the formula bar. (Command is checked if the formula bar is displayed.)

Status Bar Turns off and on the display of the status bar. (Command is checked if the status bar is displayed.)

Toolbars... Adds, removes, and customizes toolbars

Full Screen Maximizes and restores the application and workbook windows. (Command is checked if the windows are maximized.)

Zoom... Magnifies the workbook window by some specified percentage

Report Manager... Creates and prints specified sets of worksheets

View Manager... Adds, shows, and removes workbook views

Insert Menu

Cells... Adds cells to a row or to a column or adds an entire row or column

Rows Adds a row to the active worksheet

Columns Adds a column to the active worksheet

Worksheet Adds a worksheet to the workbook

Chart Displays the Chart submenu

On This Sheet Starts the ChartWizard and adds an embedded chart to the active worksheet

As New Sheet Starts the ChartWizard and adds a new chart sheet to the workbook

Macro Displays the Macro submenu

Module Adds a Visual Basic module to the workbook

Dialog Adds a new dialog box to the workbook

MS Excel 4.0 Macro Adds a macro sheet to the workbook

Page Break Adds a page break left of the selected column or above the selected row

Function... Starts the Function Wizard

Name Displays the Name submenu

Define Lets you add and delete cell and range names

Paste Lists cell and range names so that you can use one in a formula

Create Creates cell names using labels stored in adjacent cells

Apply Tells Excel to replace formula cell addresses with cell names

Note... Attaches a note to the active cell

continues

Insert Menu *(continued)*

Picture...   Adds a graphic image, or picture, to the active sheet

Map...   Activates the Data map add-in so you can chart geographical information

Object...   Adds an embedded or a linked object to the active sheet

Format Menu

Cells/Object...   Changes selected cell's/object's formatting, including its border, pattern, and protection

Row   Displays the Row submenu

Height...   Changes selected row's height

AutoFit   Changes height of selected row so that cell contents are fully visible

Hide   Hides selected row by making its height 0 points

Unhide   Unhides hidden rows in selection by increasing row height from 0 to 12.75 points

Column   Displays the Column submenu

Width...   Changes width of selected column

AutoFit Selection   Changes width of selected column so that all column entries are fully visible

Hide   Hides the selected column by making its width 0 centimeters

Unhide   Unhides hidden columns in selection by increasing column width from 0 to 8.43 centimeters

Standard Width...   Changes selected column's width to 8.43 centimeters

Sheet   Displays the Sheet submenu

Rename   Names the active sheet

Hide   Hides the active sheet

Unhide Unhides hidden sheets in the selected group

Background Adds a background pattern to the active cell

AutoFormat... Formats selected worksheet range by adding formatting for numbers, alignment, fonts, patterns, and borders

Style... Adds, changes, and deletes formatting combinations called styles

Placement Displays the Placement submenu

Bring to Front Repositions selected object so that it appears above, or in front of, all other objects on a sheet

Send to Back Repositions selected object so that it appears beneath, or in back of, all other objects on a sheet

Group/Ungroup Combines/uncombines all selected objects into a single object for purposes of formatting and repositioning

Tools Menu

Spelling... Checks the spelling of words in the cell labels of the active worksheet

Auditing Displays the Auditing submenu

Trace Precedents Draws a blue arrow to show the cells that supply inputs to the active cells formula

Trace Dependents Draws a blue arrow to show the cells with formulas that reference the active cell

Trace Error Draws a thick red arrow from cells addressed by selected cell formula returning an error and a thin red arrow to cells with erroneous formulas that address the selected cell

continues

Tools Menu *(continued)*

Remove All Arrows Erases the blue and red arrows drawn by the Auditing commands

Show Auditing Toolbar Displays a toolbar of auditing tools

AutoCorrect... Adds AutoCorrection entries and specifies how AutoCorrect works

Goal Seek... Calculates input cell value required for formula to return target output value

Scenarios... Adds and uses what-if scenarios

Protection Displays the Protection submenu

Protect Sheet.../Unprotect Sheet... Prevents/allows changes to active sheet and its contents

Protect Workbook.../Unprotect Workbook... Prevents/allows changes to workbook structure and workbook window

Add-Ins... Installs or uninstalls Excel add-ins

Macro... Runs a macro

Record Macro Displays the Record Macro submenu

Record New Macro... Adds a macro sheet so that you can record a macro

Use Relative References Records a macro's cell and range references as relative to the active cell

Mark Position for Recording Specifies where macro should be placed

Record at Mark Begins recording keystrokes and mouse-clicks

Assign Macro Tells Excel to run a macro when an object is selected

Options Changes Excel's operation and appearance

Data Menu

Sort...   Arranges a list in alphabetic order using a label or in ascending or descending order using a value

Filter   Displays the Filter submenu

AutoFilter Turns a list's headers into drop-down list boxes that you can use to selectively filter

Show All Returns a filtered list to its previous, unfiltered condition

Advanced Filter... Displays a dialog box you can use to specify filter criteria

Form...   Creates and displays a dialog box you can use to enter, edit, and delete entries in the selected list

Subtotals...   Summarizes entries in the selected list

Table...   Creates a What-if table

Text to Columns...   Starts the TextWizard, which you use to separate text into columns

Template Wizard   A data-entry template and database using an Excel workbook

Consolidate...   Summarizes ranges of values in different worksheets

Group and Outline   Displays Group and Outline submenu

Hide Detail Hides detail rows of selected worksheet range

Show Detail Unhides previously hidden detail rows of selected worksheet range

Group... Groups selected cells in outline

Ungroup... Ungroups selected cells in outline

Auto Outline Creates an outline

continues

Data Menu *(continued)*

Clear Outline Removes an outline

Settings... Creates or updates outline settings

PivotTable... Starts the PivotTable Wizard so that you can create a PivotTable

PivotTable Field... Adjusts the properties of a PivotTable field

Refresh Data Updates a PivotTable's data with the most current worksheet data

Get External Data... Retrieves data from an external database query and places the query results in an Excel workbook

Window Menu

New Window Opens a new window for the active workbook

Arrange... Rearranges the document windows into tiles or a cascading stack

Hide Hides the active document window from view so that you can't see it

Unhide... Displays a list of previously hidden windows so that you can unhide one

Split/Remove Split Splits/unsplits the active document window

Freeze/Unfreeze Panes Splits/unsplits active window. If split, freezes the window panes above and left of the active cell.

The numbered Window menu commands

Excel also lists all the open document windows as numbered Window menu commands. You can activate a listed window by choosing it from the Window menu.

Help Menu

Microsoft Excel Help Topics Starts the Windows 95 Help application and opens the Excel help file

Answer Wizard Starts the Answer Wizard so that you can ask it a natural-language question

The Microsoft Network Connects you to The Microsoft Network so that you can get Microsoft to answer a question you can't answer any other way

Lotus 1-2-3 Help... Indicates how to accomplish a Lotus 1-2-3 task in Excel

About Microsoft Excel Displays the copyright notice, the software version number, and your computer's available memory

BUTTON GUIDE

Standard Toolbar

 Opens a new, blank workbook

 Displays the Open dialog box so that you can retrieve an existing workbook

 Saves the active workbook on disk

 Prints the active workbook

 Shows what the printed pages of a workbook will look like

 Checks the spelling of words in the cell labels of the active workbook

 Moves the current workbook selection to the Clipboard

 Moves a copy of the current workbook selection to the Clipboard

 Moves the Clipboard contents to the active workbook

continues

Standard Toolbar *(continued)*

Copies formatting of the active cell to the rest of the selection

Undoes the last workbook change

Repeats the last workbook change

Sums worksheet selection, placing SUM functions in adjacent empty cells

Starts the Function Wizard

Uses the first field in a list to arrange selection in ascending value or A to Z alphabetic order

Uses the first field in a list to arrange selection in descending value or Z to A reverse alphabetic order

Starts the ChartWizard

Displays the drawing tool buttons

Magnifies or reduces workbook contents by specified zoom percentage

Starts the Tip Wizard

Displays help information about whatever you next click: a command, a piece of a workbook, or some element of the application or document window. Very handy.

Formatting Toolbar

| Arial ▼ | Changes font of workbook selection |

| 10 ▼ | Changes character point size of workbook selection |

| **B** | Bolds characters in workbook selection |

| *I* | Italicizes characters in workbook selection |

| U | Underlines characters in workbook selection |

| ≣ | Left-aligns cell contents |

| ≣ | Centers cell contents |

| ≣ | Right-aligns cell contents |

| ⊞ | Centers cell contents across selected columns |

| $ | Applies the currency style to selection |

| % | Applies the percent style to selection |

| , | Applies the comma style to selection |

| +.0 .00 | Adds one decimal place to selection |

| .00 +.0 | Removes one decimal place from selection |

| ▦ ▼ | Adds borders |

| ▱ ▼ | Colors background and fills pattern of selection |

| ▧ ▼ | Colors characters of selection |

Chart Toolbar

	Displays additional toolbar buttons for changing chart type
	Plots 2-dimensional area chart
	Plots 2-dimensional bar chart
	Plots 2-dimensional column chart
	Plots 2-dimensional line chart
	Plots 2-dimensional pie chart
	Plots 2-dimensional XY, or scatter, chart
	Plots 2-dimensional doughnut chart
	Plots 3-dimensional area chart
	Plots 3-dimensional bar chart
	Plots 3-dimensional column chart
	Plots 3-dimensional line, or ribbon, chart
	Plots 3-dimensional pie chart
	Plots 3-dimensional surface chart
	Plots 2-dimensional radar chart
	Plots default chart type, a 2-dimensional column chart

Starts the ChartWizard

 Adds and removes value axis gridlines

 Adds and removes legends

Chart Menu Guide

File Menu

New...	Opens a new, blank workbook
Open...	Retrieves an existing workbook or workspace from disk
Close	Removes the active workbook's window from the screen
Save	Resaves the active workbook as long as you've already saved it once before
Save As...	Saves a workbook the first time
Save Workspace...	Saves all the open workbooks and also creates a list of open workbooks
Properties	Displays information about the active workbook
Shared Lists...	Lists users working with a notebook and describes what they can and can't do
Page Setup...	Describes the layout of printed chart
Print Preview	Displays a window showing how printed chart will look
Print...	Prints the chart

continues

File Menu *(continued)*

Sen<u>d</u>...	Sends an Excel workbook to someone else in an e-mail message
Add <u>R</u>outing Slip...	Adds or changes the e-mail routing slip for an Excel workbook
E<u>x</u>it	Closes, or stops, the Microsoft Excel application

Numbered File menu commands

Excel also lists as File menu commands the last four workbooks or workspaces you saved. You can open a listed workbook or workspace by selecting it from the File menu.

<u>E</u>dit Menu

<u>U</u>ndo	Reverses, or undoes, the last chart change
<u>R</u>epeat	Duplicates the last chart change
Cu<u>t</u>	Moves the current chart selection to the Clipboard
<u>C</u>opy	Moves a copy of the current chart selection to the Clipboard
<u>P</u>aste	Moves the Clipboard contents into the chart
Paste <u>S</u>pecial...	Moves some portion of the Clipboard contents to the chart
Cle<u>a</u>r	Displays the Clear submenu
	<u>A</u>ll Erases the selected chart part and its formatting
	<u>S</u>eries Erases the selected chart part
	<u>F</u>ormats Erases formatting—numeric, alignment, fonts, and so on—of selected chart part

De<u>l</u>ete Sheet	Removes selected chart sheet from workbook
<u>M</u>ove or Copy Sheet...	Changes current chart sheet's position in workbook or duplicates current chart sheet
Lin<u>k</u>s...	Describes, updates, and changes selected object's link

<u>V</u>iew Menu

<u>F</u>ormula Bar	Turns off and on the display of the formula bar. (Command is checked if the formula bar is displayed.)
<u>S</u>tatus Bar	Turns off and on the display of the Status bar. (Command is checked if the Status bar is displayed.)
<u>T</u>oolbars...	Adds, removes, and customizes toolbars
F<u>u</u>ll Screen	Maximizes and restores the application and workbook windows. (Command is checked if the windows are maximized.)
Sized With <u>W</u>indow	Resizes chart so that it fills the entire window or fills half the window. (Command is checked if the chart fills the entire window.)
<u>Z</u>oom...	Magnifies the workbook window by some specified percentage

<u>I</u>nsert Menu

<u>T</u>itles...	Adds titles to a chart and chart axes
<u>D</u>ata Labels...	Adds text that describes plotted data points
<u>L</u>egend	Adds and removes legends
A<u>x</u>es...	Adds and removes horizontal and vertical axes
<u>G</u>ridlines...	Adds and removes horizontal and vertical gridlines
<u>P</u>icture...	Adds a picture to an active chart sheet
T<u>r</u>endline...	Plots a trend or regression line for selected data series

continues

Insert Menu *(continued)*

Error Bars...   Plots error bars for selected data series

New Data...   Adds a data series to a chart

Worksheet   Adds a worksheet in front of a chart sheet

Chart   Displays the Chart submenu

On This Sheet Starts the ChartWizard and adds an embedded chart to the active worksheet

As New Sheet Starts the ChartWizard and adds a new chart sheet to the workbook

Macro   Displays the Macro submenu

Module Adds a Visual Basic module to the workbook

Dialog Adds a new dialog box to the workbook

MS Excel 4.0 Macro Adds a macro sheet to the workbook

Format Menu

Selected Object...   Changes the appearance of the selection. This command name changes to reflect the selection.

Sheet   Displays the Sheet submenu

Rename Names the active sheet

Hide Hides the active sheet

Unhide Unhides hidden sheets in the selected group

Background Adds a background pattern to the active cell

Chart Type...   Selects one of the 14 chart types

AutoFormat...   Selects one of the preformatted versions available for the chart's type

3-D View...   Adjusts 3-dimensional chart's elevation, rotation, or height

Placement   Displays the Placement submenu

Bring to Front   Repositions selected object so that it appears above, or in front of, all other objects on a sheet

Send to Back   Repositions selected object so that it appears beneath, or in back of, all other objects on a sheet

Group/Ungroup   Combines all selected objects into a single object for purposes of formatting and re-positioning

Formatting data markers

The Chart Format menu also includes numbered commands for each type of **data marker** used in the selected chart. You can format a data marker by selecting the marker's numbered command.

Tools Menu

Spelling... Checks the spelling of words in a chart

AutoCorrect... Adds AutoCorrection entries and specifies how AutoCorrect works

Protection Displays the Protection submenu

Protect Sheet.../Unprotect Sheet... Prevents/allows changes to active sheet and its contents

Protect Workbook.../Unprotect Workbook... Prevents/allows changes to workbook structure and workbook window

Add-Ins... Installs or uninstalls Excel add-ins

Macro... Runs a macro

Record Macro Displays the Record Macro submenu

Record New Macro... Adds a macro sheet so that you can record a macro

Use Relative References Records a macro's cell and range references as relative to the active cell

Mark Position for Recording Specifies where macro should be placed

Record at Mark Begins recording keystrokes and mouse clicks

Assign Macro... Tells Excel to run a macro when an object is selected

Options Changes Excel's operation and appearance

Window Menu

New Window   Opens a new window for the active workbook

Arrange...   Rearranges the document windows into tiles or a cascading stack

Hide   Hides the active document window from view so that you can't see it

Unhide...   Displays a list of previously hidden windows so that you can unhide one

Numbered Window menu commands

Excel also lists all the open document windows as numbered Window menu commands. You can activate a listed window by choosing it from the Window menu.

Help Menu

Microsoft Excel Help Topics   Starts the Windows 95 Help application and opens the Excel help information file

Answer Wizard   Starts the Answer Wizard so that you can ask it a natural-language question

The Microsoft Network   Connects you to The Microsoft Network so that you can get Microsoft to answer a question you can't answer any other way

Lotus 1-2-3 Help...   Indicates how to accomplish a Lotus 1-2-3 task in Excel

About Microsoft Excel   Displays the copyright notice, the software version number, and your computer's available memory

C

D

X

Z

The manuscript for this book was prepared and submitted to Microsoft Press in electronic form. Text files were prepared using Microsoft Word 6.0 for Windows. Pages were composed by Stephen L. Nelson, Inc., using PageMaker 5.0 for Windows, with text in Minion and display type in Copperplate. Composed pages were delivered to the printer as electronic prepress files.

COVER DESIGNER
Rebecca Geisler-Johnson

COVER ILLUSTRATOR
Eldon Doty

INTERIOR TEXT DESIGNER
The Understanding Business

PAGE LAYOUT AND TYPOGRAPHY
Stefan Knorr

COPY EDITOR
Peter Weverka

TECHNICAL EDITOR
Beth Shannon

INDEXER
Julie Kawabata

Printed on recycled paper stock.